OPERATION RANGOON JAIL

Rangoon Jail from the Air

OPERATION RANGOON JAIL

by

COLONEL K. P. MacKENZIE, R.A.M.C. (*Retd.*)

With a Foreword by
BRIGADIER J. G. SMYTH
V.C., M.C., M.P.

CHRISTOPHER JOHNSON

LONDON

First published 1954
Second impression, October 1954
Third impression, November 1954

SET IN 12PT. GARAMOND AND PRINTED AND MADE
IN GREAT BRITAIN BY PAGE BROS. (NORWICH) LTD
FOR CHRISTOPHER JOHNSON PUBLISHERS LTD.
11/14 STANHOPE MEWS WEST LONDON S W.7

DEDICATION

*To my wife in grateful admiration for her heroic struggle
from September, 1939, until June, 1945;
To my daughter and my son who endured my long absence,
and
To Miss Rosalind Culhane, M.V.O., whose letter was the
first contact I had with Home*

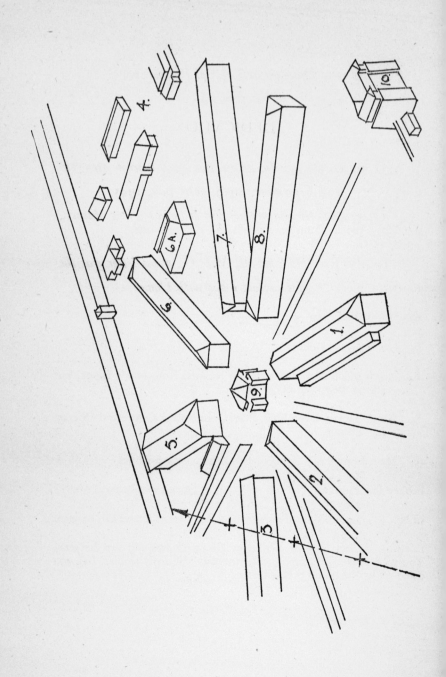

Key to Diagram and Aerial Photographs
of Rangoon Jail

1. No. 1 Block: Chinese

2. No. 2 Block: Indians

3. No. 3 Block: British

4. No. 4 Block: Punishment Cells and Empty Block

5. No. 5 Block: Solitary Confinement (*Dokbo*)

6. No. 6 Block: Americans, Hospital (Ground Floor)

6a. Hospital Kitchen

7. No. 7 Block: Indians

8. No. 8 Block: American airmen released from No. 5 Block, but still in solitary confinement

9. Water Tower. Deep Well, Bean Germinating Centre and Operating Theatre

10. Main Entrance, Commandant's Office, Guard Room

Broken line indicates where bombs fell in November, 1943.

In No. 3 Compound, slit trenches and straw roof of latrine can be seen.

Corrugated iron roof of latrine in No. 2 Compound can be seen. The roof of No. 3 Compound latrine was originally similar, but was lifted off by the bomb explosion.

CONTENTS

LIST OF ILLUSTRATIONS

We are indebted to the Air Ministry for permission to reproduce the frontispiece and the photograph facing p.188, and to the Imperial War Museum for those facing pp. 28, 29, 60, 61, 93, 108, 109, and 172.

Foreword

MY friend, Colonel K. P. MacKenzie, has asked me to write a foreword to this book in which he relates the terrible hardships suffered by himself and his fellow prisoners of the Japanese in the confines of the notorious Rangoon Jail. I am pleased and honoured to do so.

Several books have been written by Far Eastern Prisoners of War, in whose rehabilitation and welfare I have been closely concerned in the post-war years, but this one, written by a doctor, has, I think, a special interest and significance.

Fortunately comparatively few of my 17th Indian Division in Burma went 'into the bag' in the grim battle for the Sittang bridge, which gave direct access on to Rangoon, because, as soon as the bridge had been blown, the frustrated Japanese divisions withdrew to find another crossing upstream and allowed the bulk of those who had been trapped on the far bank to swim or ferry themselves across. But those who were taken, both in Burma and Malaya, went into captivity when the full tide of Japanese aggression was sweeping across South-East Asia and "England was far and honour a name". All the more credit therefore to our prisoners for their never-failing courage and humour in face of the arrogance and brutality of their captors.

Sunday, 22nd February, 1942, the day on which Colonel Mackenzie, my head doctor, was taken prisoner at Sittang, was one of those days that no one who lived through it in the 17th Division will ever be likely to forget. For weeks this so-called division, hastily re-formed in Burma from odd formations of British, Indian and Burmese troops, after the Japanese had already invaded the country, untrained and unequipped for jungle warfare and lacking any form

11

of transport and pack rations, and riddled with malaria, had been fighting a succession of rearguard actions against the advancing Japanese. They were fought and marched to a standstill and never have I seen troops so tired.

On the night of 21st February my advanced Divisional H.Q. bivouacked within a few hundred yards of the field ambulance with which 'Mac' spent the night. All night long troops and transport continued to cross the Sittang bridge in a steady stream. It was deathly quiet in the early hours of the morning as I paused at the end of the bridge to have a word with 'Mac' on my way to reconnoitre defence positions on the far bank. He asked me to stop and smoke a cigarette with him. I refused as I was trying to give up the cigarette habit. I had hardly reached the other end of the bridge before pandemonium was let loose. A flanking force of Japanese cut in from the jungle and that was the last I saw of 'Mac' for the three years which he describes in his book.

After the war I endeavoured to obtain for our ex-prisoners of war some compensation for their years of suffering. The compensation actually obtained from the Japanese in the Peace Treaty was pitifully inadequate, but we did at least establish the principle that never again must the civilised world permit helpless prisoners of war to be treated as were our men in Japanese hands.

It is as well that the British people should remember their sufferings—and, even more important, the circumstances which brought them about—and be determined that such things should never happen again.

Dolphin Square,   J. G. SMYTH
April, 1954.

Into Captivity

IN all the large cities and towns of Great Britain and in many villages and hamlets are to be found today the survivors of the Japanese prison camps. In 1939, these men were amongst the best of the nation's youth: they were splendid in physical condition and morale. Now a large proportion of them are broken in body and in mind and few indeed can be completely unaffected by the privations and diabolical and unnecessary suffering that they underwent. In telling my own story of imprisonment, I have no need to exaggerate; the facts are such that words are inadequate to do anything except convey a stark impression of part of the horror and anguish to which we were submitted. I count myself fortunate to be alive at all and to be able to take some part in the civic and community life of the ancient and historic burgh of Inverness. During the three and a half years that I was in Rangoon Jail, I despaired so often of seeing my beloved Highlands again. This cannot be a cheerful book for it is largely created as a memorial to the comrades who died around me, to those men, splendid in adversity, who never came back to tell their story.

I am a doctor and a professional soldier and have the natural reticence of the Scot. I set down this account from a sense of compulsion, from an overwhelming conviction that I must record what happened to me and to those men who shared with me a terrible experience, lest otherwise the barbaric cruelties that were inflicted upon brave and decent men are forgotten in the present fashionable attempt to represent the Japanese as a civilised and misunderstood people, who can conveniently be used to build up a bulwark against Communism in Asia and who, with a little re-education, can worthily take their place amongst the democratic nations in the councils of the world. What a fallacy this is! From my experience, I declare that the Japanese are capable of actions of which savages would be ashamed and that I see no prospect, for many generations, of the Japanese understanding the decencies that mark the cultivated man, whatever the veneer of respectability and humility they place around themselves. I write this from no sense of bitterness, but set it down as a warning based upon a conviction, obtained through observation and experience.

*   *   *

Prior to 1942, my career was not untypical of that of a regular officer in the R.A.M.C. I was educated at Aberdeen Grammar School and at the University of Aberdeen. I graduated there as Master of Arts and then entered the Medical School. After I qualified M.B., Ch.B. in March, 1914, I was appointed as House Surgeon to the late Sir Henry M. W. Gray at the Aberdeen Royal Infirmary.

On 4th August, 1914, moving quickly to participate in what we considered to be inevitably a short war, I joined the R.A.M.C. and served as a medical officer in France and in Greece. In 1919 I found myself with Grogan in North Russia. I then decided to remain in the Army with a permanent commission, and, having been accepted, I was sent upon an Egyptian Army punitive expedition against slave traders in the Southern Sudan. Then began my long association with the Far East, when I was posted to Ceylon as Adjutant to the Ceylon Medical Corps. I came home in 1924 to take the Senior Course at Millbank and qualified as a specialist in anaesthetics with distinction.

I mention here two matters in which I take some pride. I was the first officer in the British Army to administer Evipan and I have the credit of being the man who recommended that pocket handkerchiefs should be issued to other ranks in the Army, as an article of kit.

This recommendation received short shrift from the War Office on the grounds of financial stringency, as do most proposals for the amelioration of the lot of the regular soldier in time of peace, but that made it neither less wise nor less necessary.

After Millbank, I had another tour of three and a half years in India and then returned to England to take charge of the Radiological Department and School of Massage at the Royal Victoria Hospital, Netley. This period from 1933 to 1936 was my first complete home tour of duty. It was followed by a posting to Poona in 1936, but, when I contracted pneumonia two years later, I was invalided back to Britain. My sick leave being over, I was ordered to proceed to Chester on the outbreak of war in 1939, and, within a few days, I was on board the *Britannic* bound for Bombay.

The *Britannic* was in convoy with the *Duchess of Bedford* and on board was Field Marshal (then General) Sir Claude Auchinleck, returning to India. Our voyage was not without thrills and has been well described by the ship's adjutant for that voyage, Major Glover, I.A., in the January, 1940 issue of the *Journal of the United Services Institution*.

On arrival in India, I was posted to the British Military Hospital at Jhansi where the Station Commander was a certain Brigadier William Slim. I later took charge of the British Military Hospital at Jubbulpore, where there was a battalion of the King's Own Scottish Borderers, commanded by Lieut.-Col. Newbiggin, M.C., welcome companions to a Scotsman exiled from his native land for so long!

At Jhansi and Jubbulpore from 1939 to 1941, time passed pleasantly enough and often the War seemed far away. The main task was to train units of the Indian Army for the battles in Libya. The training was strenuous and we were kept busy in the hospitals, but life was quite leisurely with no real sense of urgency and there was plenty of time for tennis, golf and bridge. During the second half of 1941, the events at Pearl Harbour caused a sudden eruption of interest, but we did not realise then that these and the swift penetration of the Japanese Army through the European colonial territories in Asia were to bring the fighting quickly almost to our very doorsteps.

It was during the hot weather of 1941 that I received orders to proceed to Ahmednagar where the Seventeenth Indian Division was being formed. I was appointed A.D.M.S. of this Division, which was under the command of Major-General H. V. Lewis. We embarked upon brigade and divisional training and were under orders to proceed to the Middle East. While the Division was at Ahmednagar, I was sent down to Ceylon to carry out a medical *recce* as a part of a scheme to see if it would be possible to get an Indian brigade or division into that island for defence purposes. This was an enjoyable enough excursion but the reconnaissance was a distraction at a time when I had quite enough work on my hands, endeavouring to ensure adequate medical facilities for a division that required to be rendered fit for active service with the least possible delay.

The Seventeenth Indian Division was an ill-fated one. We were no sooner formed than we lost our Divisional Commander. On manoeuvres in the training area around Poona, Lewis slipped and damaged his knee. I took him by station wagon to the Military Hospital at Poona, where the surgical specialist agreed that he had torn a cartilage and that an immediate operation was necessary. He was replaced by Brigadier (Acting Major-General) J. G. Smyth, V.C., M.C. and, while Lewis was convalescing, the news came that we were to take part in the war against Japan and that the plans for our departure to Libya had been cancelled.

Let me be quite frank. The Division was trained and

equipped for desert warfare and was quite unsuited and unprepared for the sudden jungle rôle that was thrust upon us. Nobody was to blame for our deficiencies, the situation in South-East Asia had moved too fast to allow for anything but policies of desperation. The task that was given to us was an impossible one, but we had to face it as best we could.

Once the decision was made to throw us in against the Japanese, no time was lost. Our efficiency was not increased by the fact that two of our original brigades were taken away from us and the third brigade was separated from us until it rejoined Divisional Headquarters at Moulmein. I was in the unhappy position of belonging to a Divisional Headquarters which had no fighting troops at all with it, as it proceeded to its battle stations. First we were hustled in small parties across India to Calcutta, where the Headquarters were embarked and, after a four-day trip in a Messageries Maritimes vessel, we arrived on 6th January, 1942 at the scene of desolation that had been Rangoon Docks before the Japanese air raids had started.

We had no fatigue parties, neither was there any coolie labour available at Rangoon, so we had just to lump our baggage on to M.T. lorries and march across the city to Rangoon station. Here there were refreshment rooms, for the station was one of the most modern and best equipped in Asia, but this availed us nothing. They were all closed and deserted. We had to make do with the sandwich rations we had brought from the ship. Porters were unobtainable and again we had to load our equipment and kit on to the train. We set off for Martaban.

We arrived there next morning and, yet again, loading and unloading was the lot of the officers of Divisional Headquarters. Men and paraphernalia boarded motorbarges which proceeded across the Gulf to Moulmein. On this trip there were three air-raid alarms and, as soon as they sounded, the motor boat crews immediately made for the nearest land. It was a jittery kind of journey and we were in no mood to appreciate our first glimpse of Burma, land of pagodas, rich colourings and exquisite sunrises and sunsets.

Eventually we drew alongside Moulmein jetty on the morning of 8th January and, about 11 a.m., we were told that we were to proceed, as transport became available, to the various messes and sleeping quarters, that had been allotted to us. We were promised that we would have a high tea at 5.30 p.m., our first meal since we arrived in Burma.

Chaotic is the most descriptive adjective that I can use for the situation. It was several days before we could even assemble Divisional Headquarters.

Our officers and messes were dispersed in different parts of Moulmein. There was a Burmese volunteer brigade in the town under Brigadier Bourke. This brigade was officered by rubber planters and was badly mauled at Tavoy. During January, we were rejoined by the only one of our original brigades of the 17th Indian Division that had not been taken away from us, the Infantry Brigade commanded by Brigadier Ekin, M.C.

Air raid damage at Moulmein was slight, but the Japanese had succeeded in terrorising the civilian population. The subordinates of the municipal administration, including those of the health authority, had just vanished into the jungle. Yet the town remained under civilian control, a control that it was somewhat difficult to exercise in the absence of the appropriate officials. This question of civilian control was one of the greatest difficulties that the military faced during the Japanese drive through Burma and it was a matter upon which the Governor of Burma, that somewhat controversial figure, Sir Reginald Dorman Smith, appeared to be very sensitive. In the absence of effective authority, lawless sections amongst the Burmese were in their element and looting was of frequent occurrence.

I remember going two or three times to endeavour to interview the Medical Officer of Health in Moulmein, a certain Dr. Dass, but no relation of another Burmese medical man of that name whom I shall have occasion to refer to later. Each time I was informed by a decent little chap on his staff that Dr. Dass had gone into the jungle!

Eventually I did contact the Medical Officer of Health and asked him to show me his annual reports on the health of the population and enquired, somewhat sharply, why the sanitation of the town was in such a deplorable state of neglect and what he intended to do about it. I also requested him to take action to ensure that the latrine buckets and pails in the quarters occupied by the military were emptied. For all the co-operation I received from Dr. Dass, he might just as well have remained in his seclusion in the jungle. He naively explained that most of the employees, engaged on this work, had disappeared, that he had no hold upon them and that it was not reasonable to expect him to maintain a municipal sanitary service with no labour. He did not seem to think that his responsibility in the matter went any further than this disclaimer and, indeed, shortly afterwards, vanished altogether. I wish to pursue no particular vendetta against this Dr. Dass but his general attitude was typical of civilian control in Burma during one of the most dangerous and critical phases of the whole war there.

We remained at Moulmein until the end of January, when events forced us to evacuate the town. To Brigadier Ekin's brigade was given the task of covering the retreat from Moulmein to Martaban on 30th and 31st January. Divisional Headquarters, however, proceeded to Kyaikto where we remained until 21st February, 1942 and where two new brigades joined the Division.

Before I go on to describe the events that led to my

capture, it is necessary to get an overall picture of the position of the 17th Indian Division during February. It was impossible for a medical officer in the field to obtain this and, rather than refer to contemporary accounts of the battle by journalists, our Divisional Commander, Brigadier Smyth, who is now the Member of Parliament for Norwood, has been good enough to supply me with an account of what actually happened. He states:

"Within a short time of my arrival to take command, the Japanese invasion started and it was a case of 'all hands to the pumps'. My 45th Brigade, utterly untrained and unequipped for the task, was hastily embarked at Bombay and flung into a desperate jungle battle on the west coast of Malaya. The Brigadier was killed and the brigade cut to pieces. Shortly afterwards, the 44th Brigade was also despatched to Malaya and they became prisoners of war, without even moving off Singapore Island.

"With my Divisional Headquarters and the remaining 46th Brigade, I was ordered to Burma, where the Japanese invasion had already started. Odd units and formations were then included in my force as they became available. But the hastily improvised, so-called 17th Division suffered from several fatal handicaps compared with the highly-trained Japanese troops with whom they came in contact. First and foremost they were neither trained, clothed nor equipped for jungle fighting. They had neither pack transport, pack wireless nor pack rations, which would enable them to operate off the main road. Therefore, they could easily be by-passed by any encircling movement. In fact, the troops could only be supplied at all by a shuttle service of pooled lorries, plus the little single line of railway.

"There was in this heterogeneous collection of formations, which made up the 17th Division, a brigade of Burmese troops commanded by British officers. This brigade did not possess either the training or the discipline to stand up to the Japanese in a regular rôle. Had I been permitted to disband this Burma brigade and throw them into the jungle as scouts and skirmishers living on the country, they might have been invaluable. But questions of national prestige overrode military considerations at this time.

"Considering these handicaps, it is difficult to give sufficient praise to the troops, both British and Indian, for the grand show they put up and to the Divisional and Army staffs, who effected miracles of improvisation in manoeuvring and maintaining this unwieldy body.

"And what a nightmare the whole thing was for my good Assistant Director of Medical Services, Colonel K. P. Mackenzie!

"From our first engagement with the Japanese, it was evident that we were fighting a barbaric and ruthless enemy. Our wounded who were not evacuated were bayoneted mercilessly as they lay on the ground. Fighting their way back from position to position, the Division had held on for a week to the line of the Bilin river. But the main intermediate objective of the two Japanese divisions in their advance on to Rangoon was the Sittang river bridge, the most vital link in our lines of communication, the capture of which would give the Japanese a clear, and almost unopposed, approach to Rangoon, where it was still hoped that considerable reinforcements could be landed. For weeks the Army sappers had been converting the big iron railway bridge to take wheels and marching men, and they had almost completed this task. Such troops as I could spare from the main battle had been laid back there in a defensive bridgehead. I had known for days that fresh Japanese forces had been by-passing me at Bilin and, as soon as I was permitted to withdraw from that river line, we started to move back to Sittang with all possible speed. But the men were fought and marched to a standstill and I do not think that even after Mons or at Dunkirk have I seen troops so desperately tired. The metalled road from Martaban ended at Kyaikto, my Divisional Headquarters for the Bilin battle, and between there and Sittang there was only a bumpy track, literally feet deep in dust. It was going to be a race against time, and time was gaining on us all the while.

"That afternoon I inspected the Sittang bridgehead defences and received a message from A.H.Q. that it was considered likely that the Japs might make parachute landings on the open ground to the west of the river to try and capture the bridge from that side.

"By nightfall, my Gurkha brigade and Divisional Head-quarters were bivouacked about two miles east of the river. The bridge was now ready to take wheels and a steady stream of transport started to cross. At 3 a.m. I started to get the troops over and to move them into the positions I had selected the day before, west of the river. But, as day was breaking, whilst I chatted with Mackenzie, who was with one of his field ambulances just east of the bridge, Japanese troops were lying up in the jungle within a few yards of us. These belonged to a new Japanese division which had been moving round our flanks whilst we had been holding the Bilin river line. Within a few minutes of my leaving Mac, the Japanese burst out of the jungle. He and his comrades 'went into the bag' and the battle for the Sittang river had begun.

" A comparatively small proportion of the division was taken prisoner in this action, or indeed in the first Burma Campaign, which resulted in such an overwhelming victory for Japan and the complete withdrawal of British troops from Burma. On the early morning of 23rd Febru-ary, when the Brigadier in charge of the bridgehead defences could no longer guarantee to hold the bridge, it was blown-up and the Japanese divisions, frustrated in their attempt to

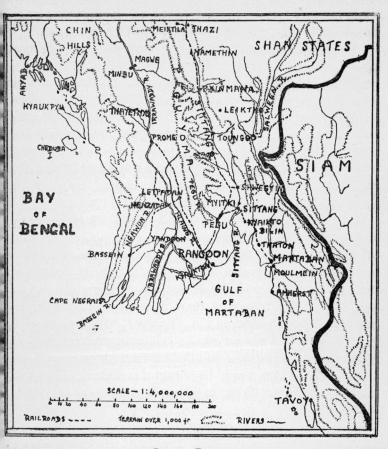

Lower Burma

make a lightning advance on to Rangoon, immediately withdrew to make a further effort to cross the Sittang further upstream. This enabled the bulk of our troops on the far side of the river to ferry themselves or swim across, where they were re-equipped and lived to fight again."

Now that the general picture is clear, my own situation can be simply outlined. My task was not an easy one as Assistant Director of Medical Services. I was faced with frustrating delays everywhere when speed was vital. As a result of the Tavoy action, the Burmese Infantry Brigade had to send back two of their medical units to re-equip and re-form. My principal difficulty, however, was that I found it virtually impossible to gauge the standard of 'fitness for their rôle in the field' of either the medical units or the regimental medical establishments.

My problems were accentuated when an order came through that all units were to hand in fifty per cent of their motor transport and were to have substituted the equivalent amount of animal transport. The reason for this order was one based upon good sense, for the country was better suited for mule transport than it was for petrol-driven vehicles. The implementation, however, left something to be desired. We lost our motor transport and received in exchange mules without saddles or harness or even head collars. The troops would have found it difficult enough to manage mules even if they had had the equipment to control them.

Some senior officers seemed to have little conception of the nature of the emergency. I visited a field ambulance commander who was in great distress because the Brigadier had just demanded a complete set of regimental medical equipment, explaining that a battalion M.O. had lost his set! I had to call upon all my reserves of patience to explain that regimental medical equipment could only be obtained through the advance depot of medical stores and that no advance depots were within ordering distance as far as I knew. I compromised by arranging for the officer commanding the field ambulance to give him a box of dressings!

Another curious request I received at Kyaikto was from a Brigadier who asked for three motor ambulance cars from one of our field ambulances to evacuate wounded. This application was brought by an officer, so I ordered the commander of the field ambulance to send a medical officer with the cars, to collect the wounded and to return with them. When the M.O. did come back, his report made it quite clear that it had been the Brigadier's intention to post one ambulance car with each of his battalions and to ignore completely the Advanced dressing station of the field ambulance and the collecting posts. It had apparently not occurred to him that this was not the rôle of an ambulance car and that he proposed to take action that would have destroyed the field ambulance as a functioning medical unit.

For some time I had been anxious to get every medical unit that could be spared back for refitting. I had already moved the Burma General Hospital out of Moulmein before the evacuation. They had only just got away in time from Tavoy without any equipment. I had also sent back from there the Burma Field Hygiene Section, the Burma Field Ambulance and the Burma C.C.S., all units which had become quite unfit for their rôle in the field. I now sent back two more field ambulances.

As the crisis of battle approached, I spent the night of 20th February with Lieut.-Colonel Gamble, I.M.S., at his Field Ambulance Headquarters in a deserted *pongyii* in the main street of Kyaikto. I was here in a good position to see how the evacuation of casualties was progressing. Casualties trickled in, all through the night. The most serious were sent by ambulance cars to Mokpalin, in convoy, and the cars were able to return before daylight on 21st February.

The brigade to which Gamble was attached moved the same day and Gamble's field ambulance, with part of a Rangoon motor ambulance convoy, was attacked by fighters on the road from Kyaikto to Mokpalin. The civilian drivers, who had been enlisted in Rangoon, found this attack too much for their nerves, abandoned their loaded ambulances and disappeared with their keys into the jungle and were never seen again by their comrades.

Here I might interpose a word or two about the terrain over which we were fighting. It is so easy, when thinking of a battle, to have in mind the kind of conditions that operate on Salisbury Plain during manoeuvres. Nothing could be further removed from the stark reality with which we were faced in those desperate days in the South-West corner of Burma. The jungle conditions made it virtually impossible for an army in retreat to maintain adequate lines of communication. The forests of teak and bamboo enabled the Japs to get within striking distance of our forces, without being observed. It was a campaign of infiltration and counter-infiltration and there was no knowing where pockets of enemy troops might be encountered. We had to bear in mind the whole time that a robust thrust by the enemy to the North West would result in our being cut off on a peninsula, surrounded by the Bay of Bengal and the Gulf of Martaban.

The situation was not a comfortable one. We were ill-equipped, we had no reliable knowledge of what was happening, even within a few miles of our base and most of the natives were indifferent about our fate, while many of them entertained feelings of hostility towards us. To the East lay the Dwana Hills and it was a cheerless thought that, unless we were captured, we were faced with the alternative of fighting our way through hundreds of miles of tree-covered undergrowth back to the pleasant province of Assam, or of becoming small, isolated bands of soldiers, trapped in a country where conditions of living were almost impossible for white men, without supplies, without ammunition and without information. Assam was our objective, but the tea plantations of Assam seemed half a world away.

I was early astir on the morning of the 21st. Kyaikto, before dawn, was a fearsome place. Troops seemed to be everywhere firing rifles, machine guns and tracer bullets into the air and across the dusty streets. This activity was caused by a few Burmese Fifth Columnists (or they may have been Japanese with Burmese clothing over their uniforms) who were letting off fireworks, looting and shooting up people in the vicinity. At daylight, this activity ceased.

I moved off with the General's Battle Headquarters at 10 a.m. across country to Mokpalin. It was an hour later that Brigadier Ekin's brigade, with Gamble's field ambulance, moved out. Our journey was fairly uneventful but the brigade was attacked time and time again by fighters.

After we arrived in Mokpalin, I went to see how the medical units were dispersed and housed. I located my office staff and D.A.D.H. and told them to move off by the train from Mokpalin that afternoon across the Sittang bridge towards Pegu. I then found the Field Hygiene Section and also ordered them to get across the Sittang bridge by road and rail.

I discovered that Lieut.-Colonel Aniswamy's field ambulance was in a *pongyi* enclosure, situated on the only eminence in the vicinity likely to attract the enemy's fire. Again here my orders were quite clear. I instructed Aniswamy to get across the bridge as fast as possible with all his ambulance, except that he was to leave one R.A.M.C. officer with a small party until Gamble's unit arrived to take over. The plan was for Aniswamy to select a site near the railway line and well clear of the bridge area, from where he could evacuate casualties on to an ambulance train, which was due during the night. One of the few fortunate things in this luckless enterprise was that all casualties had been cleared by Aniswamy's field ambulance before a message arrived that no more M.T. was to be allowed to return by the Sittang bridge. All motor vehicles were to remain on the Pegu side of the river.

It was about midnight when Gamble arrived at the *pongyii*, which we were now using as an advanced dressing station. He came in a requisitioned small four-seater car and brought with him five or six motor ambulance cars and equipment. He told me the story of the disaster that had overtaken his unit that morning. He was dead-beat, so I drove him up to Battle Headquarters in Mokpalin where he told his experiences to the Deputy-Assistant Adjutant-General.

When I was driving Gamble back to the A.D.S. at Sittang village, I saw my first Jap of the War. Gamble was sound asleep and his revolver lay at his feet, when I caught sight of a Japanese soldier, standing on the bank by the side of the road to my right, silhouetted against the sky with his rifle at the ready. I was driving without lights and it was a fairly dark night so I decided to risk proceeding. I was fortunate enough not to be observed.

By this time, I was quite exhausted. I had been forty-eight hours without sleep or food. We used to be recommended to try to do this in the days that seemed so long ago in the training area at Poona, but it always appeared to me to be rather pointless to experiment until the experience was necessary. I do not suppose that I should have felt any better if I had practised previously.

I told Gamble that he had better remain at the A.D.S., as I expected that his ambulance transport would arrive at any time. It never did, but one of his officers turned up and was captured with us.

A Solitary Confinement Cell, Rangoon Jail

A Room in a Barrack-Room Block, Rangoon Jail—taken after liberation

I snatched a little fitful sleep but was awakened before five o'clock by Burmese soldiers, from the troops who were supposed to be guarding our left flank, running about the compound. The situation seemed to be quite out of control. These soldiers had no rifles or equipment. Bullets were flying about all over the place and were travelling so low that I was forced to take up a position behind a tree. While I was sheltering there and wondering what was going to happen next, the A.Q., Lieut.-Colonel Thompson, appeared and shared half a mug of tea with me. This was the only food or drink I was to have that day or the next. He remarked that he did not like the look of things at all and my only criticism of that observation was that it seemed to me to be something of an understatement!

Thompson moved off and I called after him: "I'll be right up on your heels to Battle Headquarters in my station wagon." This was a somewhat optimistic prophesy for, when I got to the car, I found that my driver and my servant were missing and, worse than that, that they had taken the keys of the car with them.

Now occurred a lull in the firing, as I considered the position. I talked to a Royal Engineer subaltern whom I had seen previously during the evacuation from Moulmein on the Martaban side, where he was engaged in demolishing communications. He was now with a Viceroy Commissioned Officer and they told me that the Japs were very near. We decided to get down into a hollow in the ground and to await developments.

During my last minute or two of freedom, I spotted about a dozen Japs at the corner of the compound and could hear them jabbering: "Stick 'em up. Stick 'em up." We crouched lower in our hollow and the sapper asked my permission to fire. I told him not to do so. No good purpose would have been served in that situation and my revolver was locked in the station wagon. The climax came

3

when a Jap lieutenant appeared, creeping round a small building about twenty-five yards in front of us and covering us with his revolver.

"I am afraid the game is up. I will show myself and see what happens," I said.

As I stood up, the lieutenant continued to cover me with his revolver and shouted in quite good English: "Hands up. Keep them up. Come here."

When I reached him, he pulled open the two breast-pockets of my khaki shirt and appropriated the contents. Then he made me turn out the pockets of my shorts and asked me what my rank was. He seemed to understand the word: 'Doctor'. So I passed into captivity.

It may be wondered why I remained at the Advanced Dressing Station as long as I did for, if I had crossed the Sittang earlier, I could have rejoined the majority of the troops under my command and would not, at any rate, have been taken prisoner at that stage of the war. All that I can say on this matter is that I felt it was my duty to remain with the wounded in the most exposed situation. I believe that what I did was a small thing, but that it was in line with the motto of the Royal Army Medical Corps (*in arduis fidelis*).

Destination: Moulmein Jail

THE Japanese lieutenant, who took me prisoner, once he had seen what was in my pockets, turned his attention to making me understand my position. He took out a book, the pages of which were divided into two columns. There was a Japanese phrase in the left-hand column and its English equivalent was on the right-hand side. First he pointed out two phrases and made me read them out. They were: "If you give no trouble, you have nothing to fear" and "You are under my orders and will do what I tell you."

Then he pointed to the words: "Are there any more?" I replied two and called on the sapper and the V.C.O. to step forward, warning them to keep their hands above their heads. The V.C.O. was unarmed but the Jap snatched away from the R.E. officer his revolver and lanyard before going through the pockets of both of them.

We were then marched round to join the other prisoners who had been taken in the compound. Amongst them were Gamble and Major McLeod, my D.A.D.M.S., and another of my medical officers. Gamble had been captured with his driver and McLeod had been rounded up on the hilltop. In our party were about twenty men, including about a dozen Indians, who were mostly ambulance personnel.

I was offered a chair and managed to snatch my haversack and waterbottle which were lying nearby. Surprisingly enough the Japs did not take exception to my having these. It may be that, at the time, they were too greedily employed in ransacking our kit, which was their principal interest at that moment, to pay much attention.

Within a short time, McLeod and I were sent, under escort, with a note to the captain in charge of the troops in the line overlooking Sittang village. Before I went, I took care to warn all the prisoners not to attempt to escape, unless they saw a very favourable opportunity, pointing out that they would almost certainly get themselves shot or bayoneted. I heard later that this advice had been ignored. Six officers, all of whom had had their wrists tied with rope, managed to get free during a counter-attack and tried to escape. They were all shot dead, with the exception of Gamble who succeeded in getting away. I heard, after the war, that Gamble was able to resume his duties after a period in hospital at Yananyauna.

As soon as McLeod and I reached the Japanese line, the captain asked me how many big guns we had. I replied: "I do not know. I am a doctor." He then asked me to tell him what our ranks were and how many years of service we had had. When I had given him this information, he seemed content and we stood waiting upon events.

They came quickly. At about 11.30 a.m., our artillery fired mountain battery shells accurately into the Japanese line. One exploded uncomfortably close to us and killed two Japs and wounded two more. McLeod had a surgical haversack with him and we were ordered to attend the wounded. We gave first aid to them both and found that one had had his right arm very badly smashed. As it was bleeding profusely, we put on a tourniquet and a shell dressing and then told the Japanese officer that he should get the casualties into hospital. He sent back soldiers to our A.D.S. and they returned with two stretchers and carried off their comrades.

No time was lost in burying the dead. A trench was hurriedly dug and they were lowered into it and covered up with earth. There was no ceremony, except that the officer saluted the bodies briefly. He then came and sat down beside us and seemed disposed either to be friendly or to show off his knowledge.

He took out a very rough, ungridded map and showed us where the Japs had come through our flank. He gave us the information that one contingent had crossed higher up the Sittang the night before and that they were stationed well behind us on our left flank. His unit had apparently come round from Thaton and down the Mokpalin side of the Sittang river during the night and had surrounded Sittang village early that morning.

We remained in the line all that day and throughout the night. We had nothing to eat or drink. During the afternoon, the British forces mounted an energetic counter-attack and we had several times to take cover in *chaungs* (dry open ditches). We also had to hide behind trees to avoid bullets. It was an unusual and perplexing experience for McLeod and me. We were naturally anxious that the counter-attack should succeed and had hopes that we might be released in the process, yet, nevertheless, it seemed quite likely that the counter-attack would finish us off altogether. Suddenly we realised that the firing had ceased. The endeavour was over. I heard later that this counter-attack only failed by 150 yards and that the failure was due to lack of ammunition.

Between 6 and 7 o'clock, most of the Japs withdrew to a Burmese wooden building, taking us with them, and made their preparations for the night. They slept under the floor. A large green mosquito net was set up on the ground beneath the floor of the room and the captain lay down in the centre of the space enclosed, surrounded by several of his N.C.Os.

We were not so comfortable. We had our hands tied very tightly behind our backs with rough rope. One of the sentries guarding us took this opportunity to appropriate my wristlet watch. He broke the metal strap by the simple, if painful, procedure of inserting his bayonet between it and my wrist, and twisting.

I lay down with my head on my haversack but, in spite of being absolutely exhausted, I could not sleep. The tightness of the rope caused me excruciating pain. I could feel my wrists and fingers pulsating and swelling. After six hours, our hands were released, only to be tied up again in front of us. Thus we remained until morning when the rope was finally removed from our wrists, which were blistered and raw with the pressure and irritation.

About 11 o'clock that morning (23rd February) we were marched off by two relief sentries. We were given nothing to eat or drink. On the march, we passed my station wagon. I saw that it had been completely stripped. On the ground was the top of one of my leather suitcases which had been ripped off. There was no sign of any of my kit but, when we arrived at our halting place that afternoon, I saw several pieces of it in the hands of Japanese soldiers.

McLeod and I spent that night by the side of the road in a small hut. We were elevated off the ground on a small rush and bamboo platform and were left unbound to make ourselves as comfortable as we could upon the floor. It was not a very impressive bed but I immediately fell into a deep sleep, for it was a long time since I had had the opportunity of uninterrupted rest. In the next compartment of the hut to us were two I.M.S. officers and some Indian other ranks but we did not have the opportunity to speak to them.

Here I might interpose something about the way that the Japanese treated their Indian prisoners. Their aim was to try to associate Indian elements with them in an anti-White campaign. In view of the considerable amount of feeling against British rule in India and the ceaseless propaganda poured out by Indian politicians against this country, it was surprising that the Japanese were not more successful. They certainly expected to be and were profoundly disappointed to find that their efforts evoked little response, except amongst the very poorest elements of the Indian Army and amongst a few ambitious scallywags and renegades. The Indian National Army, promoted by the Japanese, was one of the biggest flops of the whole war and never became an effective fighting force. When Indians began to be taken prisoner, the Japs treated them well and put every temptation in their way to suborn them from the allegiance to which they were committed, but what success they did achieve was obtained by very different methods. They weakened the prisoners physically, mentally and morally by subtle and diabolical cruelty and then offered them a way of release by enlistment in the Indian National Army. They enlisted a force by such means, but it had little value, even from a propaganda point of view. The men of the I.N.A. hated the Japanese and, indirectly, the coercion to which they were subjected increased their respect for the British and made them realise that there were, at any rate, some benefits in British rule.

The Brigadier in charge of the Indian National Army in Burma was Lieut.-Colonel Loganathan of the I.M.S. He was a man I had known, soldiering on peace-time stations in India and was a particularly good bridge and tennis player. There was nothing vicious about Loganathan; he was a pleasant and delightful companion but, in trying circumstances and under morale-breaking pressure, he found himself unable to muster sufficient reserves of courage and conviction to enable him to defy the relentless intention of the Japanese to press him into their service. I know enough of the wickedness of the Japanese to refrain from condemning those who were their victims. We shall encounter Loganathan again as this story nears its end.

It was not only the Indians that the Japs tried to enlist

within their ranks. I have before me, as I write, a proclamation that they issued in their effort to raise a Burma National Army. Its phraseology is interesting as it gives some insight into not only the pretensions but also the conceit of the rulers of Nippon:

A CLARION CALL TO THE BURMA

ENLIST YOURSELF IN THE IMPERIAL ARMY AS 'HEIHO'

CREATION OF A NEW ORGANISATION

The Headquarters of the Imperial Expeditionary Army in Burma is creating a new organisation called 'Heiho' to which all Burma youth are allowed to join. The idea of creating such an organisation is to recruit the youth to attain divine principles and crack standard that is befitting an army on similar lines that are prevalent in Imperial Nippon. Besides there is an opportunity for all unemployed youths in Burma which should be taken advantage of.

'Heiho' is a patriotic youth organisation which is to be adapted and trained by the Nippon Army on parallel lines to that of an organisation of the divine and crack army of the Nippon Empire which is unrivalled on earth.

That was all in the future but it was significant that, from the earliest days of our captivity, the Japanese took elaborate precautions to maintain contact between Asiatic prisoners and British prisoners at a minimum. Quite clearly, a good deal of thought had been given to the question of creating quisling forces in British territory, even before the war began. Those Indians in the next compartment were separated from McLeod and myself, not accidentally, but deliberately as part of a well thought out act of policy.

After we had had a good night's rest, the next day was somewhat more encouraging. In the afternnon, we were taken over for interrogation to a table under some banana trees and I was gratified to receive back my wrist watch, together with my money and some photographs. The interrogation was conducted through a Siamese interpreter. He was well-educated and spoke good colloquial English. I had cause to remember him during the long weary days that followed, for he showed me great kindness and he was almost the only Axis-supporter of whom, during my imprisonment, I find it possible to write that. I am sorry that I never found out his name for I should have liked to put it on record here.

The interpreter volunteered, once he had finished his task, to take me over to a well to have a bath and he even provided me with soap and a towel. His goodness did not even finish there for he gave me a British officer's worn bush shirt, a sample tube of tooth paste, a packet of ration biscuits and a tin of Ideal milk. No doubt he obtained these from the 'stores', in which my field kit had found a home! We managed to get hold of some hot water in a mess tin and McLeod and I made a meal off the biscuits and washed it down with a mixture of the Ideal milk and hot water—our first meal since capture.

This interlude put fresh heart into me. It is wonderful in the tropics what a bath and a hot drink can do for a tired, dirty, hungry and disappointed man. Everything now looked more cheerful and I faced the future with mild optimism, little realising that what I had gone through was as nothing compared to the tribulations that were to come.

The next day was 24th February. I am certain about these dates for I kept a 'diary' until the end of August. This I did on a scrap of paper on which I wrote with a stub of indelible pencil. This paper I kept with me all through my imprisonment, concealed in my mess tin. I only wish that it had been possible to continue this 'diary' throughout my imprisonment but, after we arrived at Rangoon Jail, no writing material of any sort was available for long periods.

On this day, McLeod and I were marched to a bivouac

camp where we joined nineteen British other ranks from the 17th Indian Division. It was stimulating to see some familiar faces: it seemed an eternity since we had been in contact with our fellow-countrymen. I was quite unreasonably cheered when one of the men (he died later in Rangoon from beri-beri) called out: "Bad luck, sir. So they got you too." Even recognition can be a precious thing in alien and hostile surroundings.

I now lost sight of McLeod for a time. He was taken away I knew not where, and I became the only British officer amongst the small contingent of twenty British soldiers. I was made the special responsibility of a Japanese medical corporal, Eilsichi Suzuki by name. Under different circumstances, I think I could have made something of Suzuki. He had the Japanese failing of inferiority complex in his relations with me. It was a most extraordinary thing the way that this failing afflicted all the Japanese with whom we came into contact, with perhaps the exception of that sadistic devil in human form, Captain Coshima, of whom I shall have so much to say later and who will always be War Criminal Number One for me and my comrades. But then no normal rules of behaviour could be applied to Coshima. The reasons for his brutality, his inhumanity and his swinish behaviour would have, I am certain, baffled the most 'enlightened' psychiatrist. The average Jap, however, could not make out whether we were laughing at them or whether we regarded them as supermen or just as the lowest form of animal life. In their bewilderment, they were prone to hit out blindly, while they held the upper hand. We paid dearly for their lack of discernment.

I remained three days at this camp and then, together with the B.O.Rs., I set off for Kyaikto in the late afternoon of 27th February. These three days were very instructive, for Suzuki took me on his medical rounds with him. There was no Japanese doctor to attend to their troops and they had to rely upon the corporal for any treatment that they wanted. He visited several detachments and I saw my first cases of the disease that was to become so familiar to me—beri-beri. The illness was known amongst the Japanese as *kakke* and Suzuki had a quite simple, if not very effective, treatment in dealing with it. He would sterilise a 20 c.c. syringe and needles in the small lid of an aluminium mess tin and give his patients a 10 c.c. injection of vitamin B intravenously—this in the field!

If one could have viewed it philosophically, the journey to Kyaikto was not without interest. It is not often given to troops to go over a battlefield so soon after capture as we did. I saw the whole battlefield from Sittang to Kyaikto within a week of the Japanese victory at Sittang. We passed the ambulances of the Rangoon motor ambulance convoy exactly where the drivers had abandoned them, when they took to the bush. We saw mules with their legs in the air, their bellies distended through decomposition and on the point of bursting. Many dead Indian soldiers could be seen lying at the side of the road, dead in their equipment, as they had fallen. The Jap guards went through a pantomime every time we passed dead bodies. They looked at the bodies and then at each other, smiled and put their fingers to their noses. The smell was somewhat obnoxious, but this particular method of indicating it might have been a religious ritual from the methodical way in which the Japs behaved.

The Japanese showed their peculiar appreciation of hygiene by the way in which they treated enemy dead. They were meticulous in burying their own dead with the minimum of delay, but they did not seem to think that it mattered if Indian or British dead men lay about indefinitely, contaminating the atmosphere.

Another thing we were able to observe before we reached Kyaikto were some of the derelict vehicles of Brigadier

Ekin's Headquarters, together with the ransacked mess of the unit. Some vehicles were ditched; some had been set on fire but were in comparatively intact condition, while others were completely burnt out. The Brigadier's station wagon, however, seemed to be quite unharmed. It stood on the side of the road and his flag was still flying, as we passed.

When we neared Kyaikto, we were halted amongst some Burmese huts. Here we underwent a cursory examination and then the Japanese thought to have one of their pointless practical jokes with me. In the dark, I was escorted into an upper room, where, unknown to me, the planking had given way. The inquisitive little Japs swarmed up the wooden steps after me to see how I would get on in the room and, with their weight and mine, the floor collapsed completely and I was precipitated on to the ground ten or twelve feet below. Nobody would have worried if I had been hurt but, fortunately, I landed on some rubbish and no damage was done—except to my dignity.

By this time our party looked and smelt a sorry crew. Our bodies, our clothing and even our small packages of kit were offensive to the nose of the least fastidious. Nothing else could really be expected. We had had a week of sleeping rough in the open and in dark Burmese bungalows and had become the victims of lice and bed bugs. Nor had we escaped the attentions of the ubiquitous mosquito.

However, Kyaikto brought some improvement in our physical condition and to me it brought mental relief too, for I was allowed to do a little medical work.

After the incident when I fell through the floor, I was taken to the Jap guard room and quite comfortably housed for a couple of nights in one of the lower rooms there. On the first morning I was shown some Indian and Gurkha troops and told to attend those of them who were wounded.

One or two of the Gurkhas were in a bad condition, but bore their afflictions with all the fortitude for which these splendid Nepalese soldiers are famous. They had septic wounds covered with filthy dressings or no dressing at all. I had nothing to offer them except my field dressing and I did what I could with this, but I was only too conscious of the inadequacy of my treatment. I had no drugs or medicines of any sort and, when I told the Gurkhas to keep their wounds clean, I realised that this was hollow advice, for they could only get water by the grace of the Japanese. One Gurkha lad, of perhaps eighteen or nineteen, had a fractured humerus and I made a splint for him out of a piece of packing case.

The third day I was transferred to a commandeered Burmese bungalow near the railway station, where there were Indian and British prisoners, under the charge of a Japanese lieutenant named Sato. Sato was not one of the worst Japs I met and he told me that the army of Nippon believed in solitary confinement for all officer prisoners. At least he tried to tell me this but I missed his point, for he used the word *solitaire* and I could not think what he was driving at. In view of this misunderstanding, it was a mystery to me why Sato was at such pains to explain to me that I must remain in a small room with iron bars on the windows and with no furniture and only a small piece of matting on the floor. He insisted that I was only to emerge with his permission or, if escorted by one of the sentries, to have a bath in the open or to visit the lavatory. It was such a relief to have a bath that I did not worry unduly about the conditions that were imposed before I had one. Sato also detailed one of the B.O.Rs. whom he addressed, for some reason best known to himself, as Mr., to bring me my rice twice daily and to fetch a ration of boiled water for me.

Rice was perhaps the greatest of the minor tribulations of my imprisonment. I remember, almost as soon as I was captured at the age of fifty-one, how the thought flashed through my mind that I should now have to live on a rice diet. This may well seem to some people a triviality to think about at such a time, but to me it was a matter of genuine concern, for I never could, from childhood, eat rice-puddings or ground rice in any form. I survived the shock pretty well, however; far better than some of my fellow-prisoners, who had to make a conscious effort to force the rice down their throats and then very often could not digest it but vomited it up almost immediately.

Sato was anxious that the prisoners should leave Kyaikto a credit to himself. He came in every evening I was at the bungalow to speak to me and sometimes gave me what was left of his supper or a cigarette. He would squat down on the mat beside me and try to explain the purpose of morning and evening roll call. He used to get the prisoners out on the road and attempt to get them to number off in Japanese, according to the official phrase book. None of us paid much attention to this exercise at the time: it would have been better if we had, for it might have saved us from many a terrible beating in Rangoon Jail.

The Intelligence sent for me one afternoon and put me through a further interrogation. I was handed an Indian Army List and I saw that the names of certain officers were underlined in red ink. I was asked if I knew these men. "Some of them," I replied cautiously. They then questioned me about the initials of the two Brigadiers in the 17th Division, saying that they already knew all about Brigadier Ekin. I was surprised into making the remark: "Oh, has he been captured then?" but received no reply. Of course, I knew the initials for which they were seeking but I told the Intelligence officers that I had no idea of them and that I had most certainly no wish to mislead my captors. They accepted this denial.

As it was now past our meal time, I ventured to point out

that I should get no supper as a result of this investigation. This was a profitable move, for an orderly was sent away to fetch me a tin of condensed milk, a packet of Shakapura biscuits and a carton of ten cigarettes. As the Intelligence people also gave me cigarettes during the questioning, it was obvious that they wanted some special information from me. I was equally determined that they should learn nothing of value and made my answers as short and evasive as possible.

On the afternoon of 5th March, the party that had come to Kyaikto with me was reassembled and bundled into a captured British lorry. There were twenty-two of us on board altogether—nineteen B.O.Rs., myself, Lieutenant Sato, the driver and two Japanese sentries. We had no information where we were going but suspected that we were bound for Moulmein Jail. We were on the road for more than twenty-four hours and there was plenty of time for reflection. I well remember looking at my companions and thinking how pale, haggard, starved and anxious they seemed to be. I wondered, as a doctor, how long they would last in the conditions of an Oriental prison. Much that happened then has been crowded out of my mind by subsequent events, but three of these same men, at least, Sergeant A. Smith of the Duke of Wellington's Regiment, Private Thompson of the same Regiment and Sergeant W. Handsell of the K.O.Y.L.I., marched out of Rangoon Jail with me on the glorious afternoon of 25th April, 1945.

We had frequent stops on the road. The Japs blamed this on carburettor trouble and we were content to tumble out of the lorry and rest at the side of the road until they put it right, secure in the knowledge that what they were really encountering was glycerine in the petrol, placed there by our troops before the lorry was abandoned. The journey was quite pleasant, a real calm before the storm. We had two halts for meals on the second day and Sato allowed us to purchase some *juggaree* and a large quantity of pork quite cheaply. We were able to boil the pork, when we cooked our rice at the midday halt and thus had plenty of sweet hot water.

As we approached Martaban, we were halted by a Jap detachment at the roadside and were given some hot tea. Later we were ferried over from Martaban to Moulmein, where we spent the night on a godown floor at the docks, among the bed bugs, mosquitoes, dirt and kapok cushions of the Irrawaddy Flotilla's pleasure steamers.

The hour of decision came next morning. We had not been informed that we were to enter Moulmein Jail, although by this time none of us had very much doubt in our minds about this. After we had breakfasted on rice, a few spring onions and some very questionable water, however, we were marched to the Circuit House. This had been one of our Divisional Headquarter's Messes but was now the office of the Japanese Commander of the town. Here our suspicions were confirmed and we learnt that we were to enter Moulmein Jail.

We marched there under Sato and when we passed a Burmese coffee shop, he told us to fall out and to get some coffee and biscuits remarking: "It is the last drink of coffee you will have for a very long time." I think it was at that moment that the awful vista of prolonged and indefinite imprisonment came into my mind. Up till then I had been living from day to day, but I felt that I was now about to enter a place, which had gates that would shut behind me, separating me from all that I had known and loved. There was not much time to be introspective, however. We finished our coffee and biscuits, bought a few cheroots and proceeded on our way.

It was on 6th March, 1942 that we marched into Moulmein Jail.

No. 3 Block Hospital—a drawing by Pte. G. A. Ratcliffe

Medical Officer's Armlet, Identity Disc and Prison Number

Moulmein Jail

THE name of the town of Moulmein was immortalised by Kipling in *The Road to Mandalay*. It conjures up in the mind the picture of hot, drowsy, Eastern days and exotic Oriental ladies, waiting to satisfy and amuse. That *was* my conception; today it is very different. The association that now comes when I hear the word Moulmein is of an indescribably filthy prison where the mechanism of civilised behaviour had started to break down, a place that was permeated with an omnipresent stink of body odour, urine and excreta, where men lay rotten with beri-beri, dysentery and jungle-sores.

Yet Moulmein itself is a pleasant enough place, situated on the Gulf of Martaban and in that leg of Burma that shoots down into Siam. It is an old-established military cantonment and seaport. Its great disadvantage is the very heavy rainfall experienced there, but the rain brings with it a luxuriance of colour and vegetation that compensates considerably for the discomfort. It is the centre of the Burmese shipbuilding industry and has a thriving trade exporting timber, rice, cotton, ivory, wax, lead and copper. The jail there was a comparatively small one but it shared the characteristic of most Eastern jails in that its prisoners included a large proportion of men who were afflicted with infectious and contagious diseases.

The Japanese, however, found no prisoners in Moulmein Jail, when they took it over. The British Administration released everybody, convicts, felons and lepers, before the evacuation, to prevent them from falling into the hands of the conquerors. We were the replacements for the criminals, but we were treated in a way that any civilised Government would have been ashamed to treat the most dastardly criminal. The captivity we had experienced before was kindness personified compared with that at Moulmein and yet it, in its turn, was an infinitely more pleasant place than Rangoon Jail.

When we were admitted on 6th March, 1942—Moulmein had been occupied by the Japs on 31st January—we were searched. We might as well have saved the money we had spent on cheroots, for they were taken away from us, as were my safety razor and its blades, although I was allowed to keep my mess-tin, haversack, water-bottle and aluminium drinking mug. When I saw that all my personal possessions were to be confiscated, I gave my watch to Sato. He had shown glimmerings of kindness to us and I thought it might encourage him to treat fairly all other British prisoners with whom he came into contact.

I had with me two packs of cards. Their history was quite interesting. I had bought them (they were stamped 'Made in Japan') as soon as we arrived in Burma and when I did so, I remarked: "They will do to play patience when I am taken prisoner." Now I lost one of them, for a sentry said he would like a pack of 'troomps' and I had no alternative but to hand them over. If I had not given one pack to him, I knew that he would have taken both and given me a 'beating up' into the bargain.

At Moulmein, there was a block of the prison for British officers and Warrant Officers, where the prisoners were kept in solitary confinement. There was a block for Indian officers and men. The officers greatly and rightly resented being housed with V.C.Os. and rankers. A third block, which was horribly overcrowded, contained British O.Rs. Among the Indians were three or four I.M.S. officers. The treatment accorded to these men showed extremely bad psychology on the part of the Japs. At this time they were desperately anxious to recruit officers of the Indian Army for their Indian National Army, yet they needlessly created resentment amongst Indian officers by refusing to give them the differential treatment that they were entitled to by their rank. There were also a few Burmese prisoners who were employed upon general fatigues and menial work for the Japs.

On the day I arrived, I was escorted over to the Officers' Block. I got an unpleasant shock immediately. I passed cell after cell, each with a British officer in it, behind the bars, and was received in stony silence. There was not a smile or a nod of recognition from anybody, although I knew several of the officers and I saw that they included Major McLeod and Captain Kilgour, an R.A.M.C. officer who had escaped by sea from Singapore with W.O. Dainly and some others in a purchased boat. I was deposited in a whitewashed cell, completely devoid of any furniture, and the gate clanged behind me. A little later an enamel plate was thrown in under the gate by a sentry and then an iron bedstead was carried in. There was no mattress nor were there any bed clothes. All that I had to cover me and to lie upon was a blanket that I had picked up at an ordnance dump near Mokpalin station, some four days after I was captured.

When the sentries left, I discovered the reason for the unnatural and uncanny silence of my brother officers. We were in solitary confinement. It was a cruel experience for men who had done no wrong to have to live together in rows of cells and to be unable to speak to each other, or only to be able to speak in furtive whispers and even then at the risk of severe punishment, if detected.

After some time, the regulations about solitary confinement were relaxed. The Camp Commandant came one day and announced that we were to be allowed to come out of our cells and to walk about in the cement passage-way and that we could eat our meals there, if we wished. We were also to be permitted to go into other cells, provided that not more than two men were in one cell at a time. Under this relaxation, we soon found our way up the wooden staircases at each end of the block and on to the upper story, which had a wooden floor and where there was an enchanting view of the Bay and the trees and the pagodas around. What a contrast there was between the natural, lush beauty of Burma, the land of lazy colour, of passion fruit and ever-green and light blue periwinkles, of peaceful indolent people, and the darkness, wretchedness and sordidness of its jails. A further advantage of the upper story was that we were to some extent out of range of the smells of the prison, but we had to be back, locked in our cells, by 7 p.m.

We had two meals a day. In the morning we had boiled rice and beans with no salt and in the late afternoon (the time was irregular) we had some more boiled rice with perhaps some vegetable marrow or pumpkin and red chillies in a vegetable stew, again with no salt. For drink, we only had the contaminated water from the well and no provision at all was made for boiling it or chlorinating. Gone were the days of iced, sweet drinks, of gin and tonics and of sipping John Collins's, with electric fans rotating overhead.

The toilet arrangements were about as crude as they could be. We were allowed one enamel commode or petrol tin between two men. When these 'benjou pails' were made from petrol tins, they were extremely uncomfortable, for the edges were jagged and it was impossible to sit down upon them. These pails had to be emptied into a pit at first, which was in a cabbage patch adjoining the block, but afterwards the Japs decided to fertilise the *brinjal* plants in the garden. We had then to dig small holes among them and empty the contents into the holes daily. This was only done once a day before breakfast and we were given a petrol tin full of water to clean and 'disinfect' the receptacles. We had no brushes so the difficulty of the task is clear, especially as the diseases causing diarrhoea were epidemic amongst us. When we had finished our task as a sanitary squad, we were given a mugful of water to clean up ourselves and then we had to fetch and eat our breakfast. It was quite an effective means of moderating the appetite!

The Burmese prisoners had the job of bringing in water from the wells and filling up four or five chatties and one six-gallon drum. This was all the water that we had to wash our dishes and our bodies except that, once a week, we were marched to one of the other compounds for a bath. Here there was a long cement communal bath and we drew our own water to fill it to a depth of four or five inches. One day the Japanese issued tiny towels, although there were only enough for a few of us to have one. I was fortunate enough to participate in this issue and I was allowed to keep the towel.

Later we were marched out of the prison for baths. We were taken to a well in a Mohammedan temple, and there, alongside Indian prisoners, we were permitted to wash our bodies and any clothing that we might have. Many of us had no soap at all and I only had a small piece of a shaving stick which I managed to eke out for several weeks. These visits were something of an occasion for, after our ablutions were performed, we were given one cheroot between five or six of us and smoked it by squatting down in a circle and drawing alternatively. Later we succeeded in buying some cheroots from the Burmese water carriers at inflationary prices and some of the Indian prisoners sold cheroots to us also. They were able to obtain them sometimes, for they had opportunity of doing a little business with the local Burmese when they were marched to the docks to unload cargoes or perform coolie labour without pay.

I was placed in a dilemma by the action of the Camp Commandant in inviting me to take dinner with him and with the camp staff on three occasions. I certainly had no desire at all to eat with any Jap. I went with very mixed feelings, for I did not wish to be treated any differently from any other prisoner. I hoped to be able to obtain concessions and, although this was not appreciated by some of our officers at first, they came to respect my reasons. I had a good deal of pressure brought to bear upon me to make impossible demands but I resisted this, for it was my view, and I am still convinced that it was the right one, that, by pitching our requests too high, I might antagonise the Japanese and make impossible even the slightest ameliora-tion of our condition.

The justification for my attitude can be found in two inci-dents. When I was laid up with dysentery, Lieut.-Colonel Power of the Dogra Regiment, who was the second most senior British officer in the prison, wrote to the Comman-dant demanding Phenol or Cresol and some latrine paper. As a result, the officer prisoners were subjected to a long harangue from the Commandant and poor Power was locked in his cell for a week. We were told that everything of first quality went to the Japanese soldiers in the front line and that we were entitled to nothing. We were told that we were lower than the lowest Japanese soldier and that, being prisoners, a most disgraceful thing, we had no rights at all.

Another time, the Indians, anonymously, sent a letter to the Commandant complaining about the conditions in the jail and pointing out that we were being treated like criminals and not as prisoners of war. This caused a great stir and we had great difficulty in persuading the Japs that the letter had not emanated from us. In fact, I doubt if we should have been able to do so unless the Indians, seeing the difficulty we were in, had pluckily admitted their offence. They were placed on short rice rations for a week.

Yet, when I asked for the substitution of brown rice for the white polished rice in our rations, pointing out that many of the officers and men were developing boils, diarrhoea and the early signs of beri-beri, my request was granted, let me admit, to my complete astonishment. This change in diet only lasted for about five weeks but it did effect great improvement in the physical condition of some men.

During the time I had dysentery, I was given no medical treatment at all. It left me as weak as water. The medical officer in charge of the prison was a Bengali named Dr. Dass, who was engaged by the Japanese. Now that I am free, I should like just five minutes with this 'medical colleague' of mine. I set on record a name that has brought shame to even the lowest reaches of the profession, Dr. Dass of the Apothecary's Hall, Moulmein, Burma. The man was a charlatan and a scoundrel. He was also the worst type of hypocrite and completely inefficient in his work. He tried to give us the impression that he was our friend, but I never forgot the morning early on, when I was interviewing the Commandant, and this distasteful individual came in and, in the course of conversation, announced: "I am all for Japan. I am a Buddhist."

Dr. Dass was not even faithful to his Japanese masters, for he was quite prepared to act as an errand boy for us, if we would pay him sufficiently. He would bring us in such things as cheroots, cod liver oil and marmite at five or six times the market price. His sovereign remedies for all illness were either magnesia or tincture of cinchona. When I was convalescing from my bout of dysentery, McLeod developed dysenteric symptoms. He was treated by Dr. Dass with magnesium sulphate, but did not respond after a week or ten days. I could not stand the work of this blundering physician, in silence, any longer. I was tactless enough to point out to Dr. Dass that McLeod was becoming very weak, that he was losing weight daily and had all the signs of anaemia. I suggested that Dass might give him an injection. He said nothing then but next day announced that he was going to give him a dose of antimony. He gave him something but was careful to conceal what it was. I suspect that he injected two grains of emetine. It did McLeod no good at any rate. He felt very uncomfortable and was unable to eat at all. Within forty-eight hours, Dass gave him another injection which seemed to influence his pulse rate and made it beat very fast. After that, nature was allowed to take its course.

McLeod did not have his troubles to seek at this time. He complained to me that he was being bitten at night. Now he was one of the few prisoners who had a straw palliasse and we thought that it might be lice from this that were troubling him. Then some inconsiderate fellow prisoner mentioned bed bugs. It was a foolish thing to do, for the men were in no state to survey the prospect of bed bugs with equanimity.

I inspected the palliasse and, sure enough, I found bed bugs in it but I was not prepared to disclose this fact to anybody. The bed bug is an unpleasant-smelling, ubiquitous insect and can cause great discomfort. The men would have been very disturbed to know that they were in their midst. I, therefore, reported that there were straw weevils in the palliasse and that they were looking for blood. I recommended that the best thing to do was to put the straw palliasse out in the sun during the day and that they would then die off. This procedure was quite effective.

The unfortunate McLeod was badly bitten all over his body which added to his discomfort for he could not refrain from scratching the bites. He was, however, stout-hearted enough to struggle along and, in the course of time, he recovered somewhat and came with us to Rangoon, where he remained until the Liberation.

What happened to Dr. Dass I cannot tell. One day he collected a goodly sum of money from us to purchase extras and that was the last we saw of him. I certainly hope that he then met with his just deserts but I suspect that it was a simple case of convenient forgetfulness.

Several B.O.Rs. died in Moulmein. We were told by the Japs that the cause was dysentery but could never confirm this as we were not allowed to see their bodies.

At Moulmein, in contrast to Rangoon, British officers were treated rather better physically than were the other ranks. The first indication that we received of what was to be our common lot happened one day, when we were marching to our bath. We were horrified to see a little Jap soldier rushing at one of the British prisoners and lashing him over the back with a leather whip, because he had stumbled and allowed one handle of the refuse bin to slip out of his hand. This was the beginning of a calculated policy of brutality towards the men. Kicking and beating became ever more frequent.

The officers were not subjected to this physical maltreatment to the same extent, however, although I remember an incident in which Lieutenant Ashwell featured. He was weeding in the garden when he displeased a Japanese interpreter by a gesture. This fellow slapped him several times on the face and then took him to the Commandant, who lashed him across the shoulders with a cane and sent him back to his cell, to be locked in for a week.

The Commandant was replaced in late May and, as soon as the new one appeared, it was evident that something was in the wind. He did not trouble us unduly, except that he held frequent searches to ensure that we had no contraband. The Japs, however, began to check up on our kit and to

ensure that we had either two blankets each or one blanket
and a sewn up greatcoat, in lieu of a blanket. They also
compiled a complete nominal roll, giving the number, rank,
initials, name and unit of each man. I took little interest in
this proceeding for I was pretty low. Imprisonment in these
circumstances was not agreeing with a man in his fifties.
Following upon my dysentery, I had a series of boils and I
developed bed sores on both hip bones and on my sacrum,
through lying on the hard floor and the bare iron prison
bedstead.

Quite apart from the indignity and the mental humiliation
of being a prisoner, we were faced with a terrible boredom.
There was just nothing to do, day after day. We had no
books and could not read, neither did we have writing
material. We were able to play cards with my one pack but
that was not much amongst so many officers. I am not
quite right when I say that we had no books, for Power,
who was a devout Anglican, had managed to retain a
Prayer Book. Each Sunday morning, after we were
released from 'solitary' in Moulmein, either Power or I
conducted a Service for the British officers. It was a simple
act of worship and of faith and I believe that it did strengthen
the ties that bound us together. We finished each Service
by singing the National Anthem and it was a moving
experience to stand with a group of men who had lost all
touch with their native land and who, indeed, had no
assurance that they would ever again see their homes, their
families and friends while they lifted rugged voices in the
old familiar words: "God Save Our Gracious King". At
such moments, it was inevitable that memories of happier
days should come crowding into the mind and these
Services were, I believe, quite apart from their religious
significance, an inspiration and a morale-raiser to us all.
Amongst the officers, the Services continued until the last
few months of our imprisonment in Rangoon, when the

attitude of the Japs made it impossible to continue open worship any more. At Rangoon Jail, too, Services were arranged for the men by Brigadier Hobson. Except for one short period, of which I shall tell later, we had no clergyman or minister with us. The Services were a spontaneous response to a fundamental need in our conditions of adversity.

My boils did not get any better and Captain Kilgour resorted to radical surgery. I had ten boils in all, including one on the thigh, one on the chest and one on the left breast. Kilgour opened one in each axilla with a borrowed, very blunt scalpel. This was an extremely painful little operation and, suffering as I was from vitamin B deficiency, I was quite unable to take it in my stride. Night after night, I lay on the bedstead, with no mattress, sleepless, weak and in agony. It is little wonder that the intense administrative activity of the Japanese aroused little curiosity in my mind.

This activity culminated on 25th June—a day of drenching rain. Without previous warning, we were paraded with our kit, told to get into lorries with the B.O.Rs. and, under escort and accompanied by the prison Commandant, were driven down to one of the jetties at Moulmein. I was really in no condition to travel. I could manage to walk but, when I tried to climb into a lorry, it was too much for me to accomplish. Other officers had to lift me in.

We were embarked upon a three thousand ton cargo boat. The journey was like some horrible nightmare. We were all crammed into the after-hold, which was packed around with moist sacks of *juggaree* slabs. The atmosphere in that hold was as thick as anything I am ever likely to experience. There was little ventilation and, quite apart from the dirt and the smells of saturated sticky bags, human sweat and excreta, many of the men were very ill. We only had four empty five-gallon tins as latrines and, with men suffering from almost continual diarrhoea and having no control over their movements through beri-beri, exhaustion and dysentery, the condition of the hold was soon absolutely revolting. After some hours, I felt absolutely 'all in' and I requested that I should be allowed to spend the night on deck with the stretcher cases. I also made the same request on behalf of Power. The Commandant allowed me to go up with my kit but insisted that Power should remain below. I passed a fair night, for even the persistent rain was infinitely better than the conditions in that hold.

It was still raining when on the next day we pulled alongside Rangoon Docks, at a berth near the Shwe Dagon pagoda. We disembarked and marched through the city, as best we could, pursued by millions of flies, attracted by our sticky *juggaree*-soaked clothing, to the Rangoon Central Jail. I had reached the place where I was to spend the remainder of my imprisonment.

Hopes that Disappeared

IT is a strange thing but those of us, who arrived at Rangoon Jail on 26th June, 1942, did so in a mood of qualified optimism. We were in poor shape physically, but we believed that the change from Moulmein would be one for the better. We were glad to leave that place with its unhappy experiences and we were heartened by the know-ledge that the weather would be pleasanter at Rangoon. Moulmein with its torrential rain made our arduous imprisonment even more depressing than it would otherwise have been. We knew that Rangoon was a good deal drier and this cheered and comforted us.

Additionally, the glimpse that we had of the outside world during the transfer was stimulating, in spite of the grievous conditions of our journey. In prison, the temptation is to submit to a feeling of helplessness and hopelessness, a belief that one is living in a small and confined world and that nothing much can happen anywhere else that is of any consequence. In this frame of mind, even passing for a brief time through the streets of a conquered country, as prisoners of the conquerers, was a salutary experience. It brought us into touch with a reality, which we had almost ceased to believe existed.

The uplift accomplished by the change was an excellent thing, even although our hopes were soon to be dashed and we were to experience worse things than we had already undergone.

Rangoon has been described as the 'loveliest city of Burma' and it has much to commend it to those in search of beauty in the Orient. One hundred years ago it was but a small fishing village but, by the time of the Japanese occupation on 20th February, 1942, it had grown to be a city of more than half a million people of many nationalities and creeds. During the previous thirty years the growth of Rangoon had been phenomenal: in 1911, the population was under three hundred thousand, by 1931, it had risen to over four hundred thousand and, in the following ten years, another hundred thousand were added.

When the Japanese invaded Burma, there were nearly twice as many Indians in Rangoon as Burmans, in fact, nearly half the total population of the city was Indian. There were also thirty thousand Chinese and the European and Eurasian population was in the neighbourhood of fifteen thousand.

The city is dominated by the great Shwe Dagon Pagoda. It is higher than the dome of St. Paul's Cathedral and the gleam of its beautiful gilt exterior in the harsh, Burma sunlight can be seen for miles around. The Pagoda is the most frequently visited place of worship in the whole of the East. Buddhists claim that the Shwe Dagon Pagoda was first erected in 588 B.C. and that it stood only twenty-seven feet high. They believe that the original building is still the foundation upon which the present colossal edifice has been established and that the great height has been obtained by repeated casing with an outer covering of bricks, several feet in thickness.

The great importance of Rangoon is as a port. It is by far the biggest port of Burma, the docks being twelve times as large as those at the second port, Bassein. The business part of the city lies between the Irrawaddy and the railway line. Here also is Commissioners Road and in Commissioners Road is Rangoon Jail, a stark ugly collection of buildings which comprise one of the largest jails in the British Empire, having, in normal times, accommodation for some three thousand prisoners. We shall later consider in some detail the layout of the jail, but it is worth recording here that the external appearance is such as to cause some apprehension to the potential wrong-doer and to send a shudder down the spine of a sensitive architect. The system of separate blocks served the purpose of the Japanese well, for it enabled them to carry through a policy of segregating prisoners of different nationalities, comparatively easily.

When the gates of the prison clanged behind us, we were halted and had our names and ranks checked and were issued with small cards. I have my card to this day. It bears the inscription 128, which was my first prison number.

The parade was in charge of a Japanese corporal, who could speak some English and who was second-in-command of the jail. He established his relations with me right away by coming up to me and ordering sharply: "*Teisa* (Colonel). Attention." I did not like the look of this N.C.O., neither did I relish his manner, but I came to attention as smartly as I could and quickly warned the others to do likewise, when they were addressed. I was too late with my advice, however. While I was speaking to the officers, some of the prison staff attacked them, slapping their faces and kicking them in a most brutal manner. Foremost amongst the persecutors was a tiny savage, whom we came to call the Little Lance-Corporal. He went about his punching and kicking with gusto and caused two of the officers to faint. He and his colleagues were surveyed with approbation by the Jail Commandant, Captain Coshima, who stood near the entrance in brown field boots and soft khaki cap, with a sadistic smile on his face.

I never thought, when I lived under civilised conditions, that I should rejoice unfeignedly to hear of the death of another human being. When, however, the news came a few months later that the Little Lance-Corporal and two others of the prison staff had been killed by a British light bomb dropped just outside the main gate of the prison, the news brought to me a sensation of pure, unalloyed joy. Even the fact that the bombing resulted in further savagery towards the British and American prisoners could not completely wipe out our feelings of bliss.

When this performance finished, the N.C.Os. and men were marched away to barrack rooms and the officers to solitary confinement. I now had a piece of luck. Neither Captain Tothill of the Baluch Regiment nor I were able to keep up with the main body of officers on the line of march, owing to our physical condition. Tothill had received several nasty bullet wounds, including two in the lower jaw, and these had been disgracefully treated by the iniquitous Dr. Dass at Moulmein. He and I were helping each other along when, quite accidentally, we turned into the wrong block. Here we were greeted by a small party of British officers, who had arrived at Rangoon some three months before. They were Captain Henstock of the Indian Cavalry, Captain 'Geordie' Fullerton of the Royal Scots Fusiliers, Captain Colgan of the Royal Inniskilling Fusiliers, Captain Brian Western and Major Nigel Loring of the Indian Cavalry and Captain 'Bunny' Bunten of the Cameronians. We had time for a short chat and, after Joe Colgan had seen my bed sores, he did me an inestimable kindness. He gave me a prison mattress of coir, that had been left over from the civilian occupation of the jail.

We did not have long with these officers for a sentry was sent to look for us and, as soon as he found us, we were bundled unceremoniously off to 'solitary'.

The mattress was not only a good friend to me. It was also a great boon to us all. It provided me with a little comfort and became for my comrades a storehouse. I had not been in 'solitary' long when Coshima came in, with his Siamese interpreter, and drew attention to the mattress. I showed him my bed sores and he agreed that I should be allowed to keep it—it was in any case no use to him.

A Street in Rangoon

The Schwedagon Pagoda

The Moulmein party of officers remained in 'solitary' for seventy-seven days. It was 8th September, 1942 before we were allowed to become routine prisoners. Some strange things happened while we were there. We were continually disturbed, both by day and by night, by Nip sentries. They would come sneaking along the corridors, very often in rubber boots and would stop outside the gate of a cell. The occupant of the cell would then have to bow to the sentry in Japanese fashion. This was a particularly subtle form of torture, for it prevented us from getting any proper sleep. If one did not immediately rise and bow as soon as the Jap appeared, however silently he might have approached, one was beaten-up. I remember, on one occasion, two officers in cells not far from mine were caught asleep by a sentry. He roused them, took them out of their cells and ordered them to slap each other until one collapsed. The winner was then knocked about by the sentry until he too collapsed.

Another favourite trick of the sentries was to enter the cell and search an officer's kit. They would turn his bed upside down, steal any little luxuries he had been able to purchase and go away, laughing.

The Little Lance-Corporal was, of course, foremost amongst these tormentors. His speciality was to approach a prisoner and shout at him: "*Kio*", the Japanese word for 'today'. This was meant to convey to the prisoner that he was to reel off the day of the week, the date and the month of the year. Failure to do so resulted in a beating or a kicking. After one or two experiences of this sort, I used to write the appropriate information in small capitals on the wall of my cell, near the gate, so that I could rattle it off quickly, whenever asked.

During July, I was removed from 'solitary' to take the place of Brigadier Clive Hobson in another block, known as Punishment Cells. I shall have much to say of Hobson, as this story continues, but the first time that I saw him was as we passed each other as we exchanged blocks. We were, of course, unable to speak but we did wink at each other. I was no better off in the Punishment Cells for confinement was solitary there also. I remained there until the end or August, when I was returned to 'solitary'. There was no means of artificial lighting in these cells.

It was during these seventy-seven days in Rangoon that we first experienced the Japanese mania for ordering their prisoners to write essays. This served the dual purpose of obtaining from officers information on military subjects and of making them record their impressions of certain events. One of the first subjects I was given was on 24th July, 1942, when I was handed a piece of paper with the following on it:

Question. "Apply your stock of knowledge to your professional study."

I was told that my reply would be collected on 27th July and I, therefore, attempted to clarify the question by sending the following note to the Commandant: "Does this mean: 'Apply my medical knowledge of rations as issued, to their uses as aids in feeding troops or patients in hospital?' Could I kindly be given a reply as I am not very clear as to what the question has reference?"

The reply of Coshima did not take me very much further. He wrote: "Yes; it means all your knowledge of medical science and medical movements in the field." I have this correspondence before me, as I write now and it is no clearer to me today what was wanted than it was at the time.

However, I knew that I should have to write something so I wrote sixteen pages of nonsense about preventive measures against typhus, cholera, tetanus and diphtheria; about the care, collection and treatment of sick and casualties; about the feeding of troops, composition of diets, carbohydrates, vitamins, fats and salts; and about the great difference of diets required by peoples, dwelling in temperate and tropical climates, with particular emphasis upon the effects of a rice diet on Europeans.

My eyesight was very bad at the time I wrote this essay and I was suffering from dengue fever. I had, of course, no books of reference to assist me and it had to be written with the paper on my knee. I took the opportunity of recording the impossibility of completing a satisfactory essay under these conditions and waited developments. Next day I was told that the essay was too short and I had once again to sit down on the cement floor of my cell, with sheets of monsoon rain blowing across the paper, and complete another eight pages. This time, I added some information about the supply of artificial limbs and surgical instruments and about massage and electro-therapy.

On 13th August, 1942, the Japanese made their first effort to undermine our loyalty to the Crown. Each of us in 'solitary' was handed the following manifesto: (I reproduce it exactly as I received it.)

"1. The Great Japan, since she was constructed about 3,000 years ago, has never been defeated by any other foreign country, so in this war no Japanese person thinks at all that their country will be defeated nor even has the slightest fear of it.

Hakko-wo Ie-to-nasu is a sentence, quoted from the Jimmu Tenno's edict, the first Emperor, that means 'You shall cover the world by one house', that is our purpose in this war.

2. In the war 1914-1919 (*sic*) Japan observed faithfully the Japanese-British-Military-Treaty and fought hard for the allied countries.

In the conference at Versailles the reward, for the Japanese hard efforts, was too small. After the great war the British and American policies to Japan were extremely brutal. In the Washington Naval Conference they succeeded not only in compelling the Japanese Navy to adopt the ratio of the total tonnages of the Principal Battleships 5:5:3 but also to settle the limited defence area, in the west half of the Pacific Ocean, they applied much limit on Japan and hardly any on their own side.

Thus the Japanese nation burnt with indignation and determined in their minds to conquer Britain and the United States. And as soon as they determined to conquer both of these great powers Japan left the

League of Nations. Some years passed after that and the vast national resourses were stored. We can't certify that since then we observed faithfully the international treaty which was very convenient only to Britain or U.S.A. and unpreferable to the other countries. The national strength was intensified very much more.

3. When shall the present war end? That is when Britain and the United States shall surrender to Japan, or that Britain shall be wiped out of existence. Great effort and long years shall be necessary for us to destroy the British. The war was opened under expectation that the war should be continued for fifty years or a century or longer.

4. All preparation in order to destroy the British and United States were arranged very secretly with sufficient care. The strength of the nation was a secret from any country, even our own people did not know our strength and preparation, much less the foreigner. While German and French people propagated exaggerately about their Siegfried or Maginot line, Britain and United States propagated their superior power, over confidence of their strength with little regard to the training or their army. The Japanese made their very best effort to strengthen their power more and more.

There is a word among the Japanese Navy men 'Double Mondays and Fridays and no Sunday and Saturday a week' that means they have no holidays in a week. The training was so thorough, for example each pilot of the Japanese Air Force was completely trained so that he could be able to dash into funnel of the enemy's battleship with bombs loaded on the plane, thus causing instantly the sinking of the enemy's battleship at the sacrifice of his plane and life.

Nevertheless we overlooked the low estimate of the British and American side in comparison with our strength intentionally in order to throw them off their guard.

5. Thus at last war was declared on Britain and America and since the opening we have achieved many glorious victories. During the first half year Hongkong, the base of the British Empire in the Far East fell, Singapore which was called the most impregnable fortress in the world fell, the Philippines Islands were captured from the United States and the Dutch and British East Indies Islands have also been occupied by the brave Japanese soldiers. Overcoming French-Indo-China, going to alliance with Thai, now we are pressing all India. What of India? The committee of the all India national conference passed a resolution that all British must be withdrawn from India on the first of this month. In the Pacific from Aleutian island in the North to New Guinea in the South all the surface of the ocean including islands in it are under control of our great fleet and Australia is under big bombing from our Air Force.

Just three or four days ago in the sea near Australia a British Great convoy fleet was attacked by our fleet. Twenty seven ships including thirteen battleships and cruisers were sunk and 68 aeroplanes were shot down by the Japanese force. The successful fight is moreover extending.

6. Thus the war situation is developing advantageously for Japan. We are now in the state to get freely petroleum, tin and rubber, food supplies are also plentiful. Now Great Japan controls all territories which supply all necessary materials for war and the ocean's surface on which the ships transports the materials.

The British and United States Navy combined who had the advantage of being able to conquer the Japanese Navy in the ratio of 10 to 3 were so badly destroyed and decreased in strength, that their proportion will never be able to dominate the Japanese fleet.

Thus the victory in the end is firmly on the head of Japan.

7. The Germany Army have taken Sevastopol, dominated over the black sea, occupying Rostov and dashing into the Caucasus. In Africa, German and Italian ally armies are very near to Cairo.

8. If the U.S.S.R. had real power she could have attacked the back of Japan during her operations in the tropic zone, or she could also have made a counterattack to the Germans during the winter campaign, but the U.S.S.R. could not do both and she is now being routed and Germany has the store of corn and oil well districts. Inside Russia an anti-Starlin (*sic*) party is rapidly growing.

The defeat of the U.S.S.R. as well as the submission of Britain and the United States, especially the fall of Britain is now the problem of time.

9. Thus we fought and now we are surprised to see the weakness of Britain and United States, which is more than we expected first and even feel compassion for them.

We thought at first that Anglo-Saxons are a self-asserted and un-relieveable race. But seeing many prisoners in the various frontiers we reconsidered that they might understand if we explain the purpose of our war and relative merits.

That is more compatible to the spirit of *Hakko-wo Ie-to nasu* to catch the enemy alive and amend their evil ways than to make all of them perish.

10. So we want now to teach our real intention to the British and American people and relieve them from an unhappy end. That is why we intend to propagate so as to rescue Britain and United States from their fate. Naturally Japan is not a country of propaganda and its propagandists have not got much experience, so she needs some co-operation with those who have good talent in this way. That is why we want to recommend you to the Japanese Radio Broadcasting Bureau. They will pay you a salary of Rs. 500 monthly to you if you are willing to assist them.

11. The Japanese have a different idea of war imprisonment from you. Your people seem to become war-prisoners shamelessly. And your

Government also consider well of them as those who did their best. But the Japanese people think imprisonment the most disgraceful thing and prefer death. The interchange of prisoners cannot be applied to Japan. The rules as to the treatment of war-prisoners made under the restraint of the British or the United States (then the powers) should be changed according to the Japanese idea.

12. You threw down your arms and took an oath to give up all resistance, but we see some among you are not yet obedient to us in their mind and dare not co-operate with us. The war in the modern age is not decided only by the army power by total strength of the nation. In such an age it is necessary that the victory shall include the line of thoughts. Though you might think it enough to lay down your arms, we should never admit those who are not obedient even in their thoughts or spirit as a true surrender. We are mindful to dispose of such fellows as we like irrespective of life or the war-prisoner rules.

Our country is requiring of every man his best efforts in his own position in the slogan of 'Develop Power', much more she requires from every prisoner naturally his full efforts by mental or labour work.

It is arranged that almost all of you, irrespectively of being under our inspection or not, shall be engaged in constructing works of road under supervision of our soldiers.

13. Probably you used to think that the propaganda by your enemies was always advantageous to them and did harm to your country. But Japanese propaganda is a different case. You should recognise that this will rescue your country at the end from destruction.

Besides you may be afraid of any trouble that may be caused when you return home if you assist in Japanese propagation. But such fear is unnecessary, because your name and rank will be profoundly taken care of and will not be exposed and also the Japanese terms of peace shall include a term that the enemy country shall not be able to trouble in any way those who co-operated with Japan but will protect them. We shall never admit any peace if the above term is not absolutely agreed upon. We hold a firm conviction in victory.

14. So if Britain or United States are not able to comprehend the Japanese true intention and consequently remain to fight, their way is only to their grave. Moreover you should know that you may be unable to live to reach your country.

We are calling for volunteers who are willing to co-operate in this holy propaganda act of Japan so that you shall be able to rescue your nation from the ruin, quicken your chance of returning home and surely enjoy the far more comfortable life during the war in the cherry-blossoming country.

If you wish to volunteer write 'yes' and your signature, rank and prison number, if not write 'no' and the same."

This farrago, which almost certainly originated from Coshima and not from the Japanese command, in spite of its strange punctuation and even stranger phraseology, was prepared by somebody who understood at least the rudiments of war psychology. It must be remembered that it was addressed to men who were cut off from any source of information, to men who knew nothing of the progress of the war, except for such scraps of heavily-weighed information as the jailers passed on to them. It contained some statements that we knew to be true and it was impossible to disprove the truth of the others. It was obviously intended too to provide weaklings with excuses with which they could salve their consciences if they accepted the offer.

I was away from the main body of prisoners and had, at that time, no idea what they would reply but my duty was clear. I returned the answer: "No. I am bound by the terms and articles of the Geneva Convention as a doctor."

My suspicion that the document was of local origin was confirmed the following day when I was suddenly ordered to put on my khaki shirt, shorts and shoes for an interview with the Commandant. I was marched into a room on the ground floor of the prison. Coshima was sitting there at a table, wearing a white silk shirt, a pair of long jungle-green trousers and wooden shoes. This was a most unusual dress for Coshima and, with my deteriorating eyesight, I did not at first recognise him. I came to attention, Japanese fashion, in front of him and the Siamese interpreter who was sitting on his left.

"Sit down," the Commandant barked. I did so on a chair facing him. On the table between us, I saw the dossiers of the officer prisoners from Moulmein. Coshima then proceeded to give me a resumé of the document to which I had already given very careful attention. His English was not good and he had to be helped by the interpreter. When he had completed this unnecessary task, he turned to me and asked:

"Do you know that this war will last fifty or a hundred years?"

"It has never occurred to me to regard war from that point of view," I replied.

Coshima then dramatically pointed his finger at me and shouted: "How old are you?"

My reply was: "I am in my fifty-second year."

"Do you think you will live to be a hundred and fifty-two?" was the next question.

"No," I quietly rejoined, "and, if you will forgive me saying so, I don't think you will do so either."

As soon as I had said this, I realised that it was a bold utterance indeed for a helpless prisoner of war, but Coshima, on this occasion, was anxious to carry me with him. He laughed heartily—the only time I ever heard him laugh.

The dialogue continued:

"You are a doctor?"

"Yes."

"Your services, as a doctor, will not be required. We have plenty of good doctors."

"If my services as a doctor are not required, I request that I may be repatriated under the appropriate clauses of the Geneva Convention, as I am a non-combatant."

"Ho! Ho! but we do not recognise the Geneva Convention. We do not recognise international law. It is a long time since the Great Japan withdrew from the League of Nations and joined in this war with her ally, Germany."

The veneer of affability was beginning to wear thin with Coshima and, in view of the horrible leer on his face, I did not feel that this was the time to point out to him that the Geneva Convention was the responsibility of the International Red Cross and had nothing to do with membership of the League of Nations. My disquiet was growing but

I thought I would try to reason with him at least once more.

I continued: "When Japan was on our side in the last war, you observed the Geneva Convention and conformed to the Laws and Usages of War and to international law."

He replied: "The Great Japan was very dissatisfied with the poor reward she received from Britain, France and American for her help in the last war. That was the reason for her leaving the League of Nations, when she did. That too is the reason for her joining Germany in the second World War."

Coshima then picked up a piece of chalk and drew a rough map on the table of the Mediterranean Sea and the Suez Canal saying: "This is the Mediterranean. There is Cairo. There is Alexandria. This leads on to India. Today the Germans are fifteen miles from Alexandria."

He emphasised this last point by stabbing the table at Alexandria with his piece of chalk. He then sat back and waited my reaction. I ventured:

"I am very interested to hear that, for it is the first news of the war I have had since I was captured."

Coshima evidently considered that he would get no further just then for he spoke to the interpreter very quickly in Japanese and announced: "That is all. I want you to reconsider your decision. I will send for you again."

I bowed and retired to my cell.

On the morning of 17th August, we were paraded. All were there from the Punishment Cells as well as those in 'solitary'. We marched into the execution yard—a fact that did not make us feel any more cheerful. The yard was a mass of uncleared wreckage—a relic of the heavy bombing of the city when the Japanese captured Rangoon.

There were Burmese troops on our right and Indian troops faced us on our left. After an hour during which we were left standing in the tropical sun—most of us had no headdress at all—Captain Coshima appeared, carrying a steel golf-club shaft in his hand. I was told to bring the parade to attention by a Jap N.C.O. and, at attention, we remained.

Coshima stood in front of us and with a snarl, just like an animal, announced: "You have refused to co-operate, therefore I am going to punish you." He followed this up by pointing to Power and telling him to step out in front.

What had happened was this. Some of the Burmese prisoners had been promised their freedom if they would beat the British officers. The Indians had then been brought out to see the humiliation of the white men.

We stood at attention while Burman after Burman attacked Power. They each gave him a blow on the face with a closed fist or a slap with the open hand on either cheek. Some of them hit him as lightly as they dared but others took a run first to increase the force of their blow. I counted the blows and twenty-two or twenty-three Burmese hit Power before he swayed and fell to the ground. He pluckily got to his feet again but was obviously very groggy. No mercy was shown. It took eight or ten further blows to knock him out finally and he stood there, receiving them, with his face bruised and swollen and with his lips and tongue cut and bleeding. When he fell, the Japs just let him lie, a prostrate figure amongst the dust and wreckage of the yard.

Immediately Loring was called out to take Power's place. He was a short thickset man and he stood up to about thirty blows and never turned a hair. There he stood at attention, without flinching, like the Rock of Gibraltar. His defiance put fresh heart into us all. It even caused Coshima to stop the beatings, for he could see that the magnificent courage of the indomitable Loring was increasing British prestige. The Commandant shouted: "To save further punishment, I will allow you to reconsider your decisions. How long do you want?"

Captain Colgan, who was acting as parade adjutant, replied: "We have never had a chance to discuss the matter between ourselves because we are not allowed to talk in solitary confinement. May we have ten minutes?"

Coshima intimated shortly: "You can have two minutes."

As the senior officer present, I had a considerable responsibility. I told my comrades shortly that we would abide by a majority decision but that, in view of what had taken place, no jury of our fellow-countrymen would convict us of cowardice, or any breach of military discipline, whatever was decided. We were being beaten into submission.

Loring added his comments, saying that we should obviously be unable to submit to this kind of torture day after day and that it might well get worse. We decided that it might become necessary to give the appearance of some co-operation but resolved to wait upon events.

I then marched the parade out of the yard in British Army style but, before we had gone far, we were halted and recalled. A sentry whispered to me that I had omitted to call the parade to attention and to bow to the Commandant, before we marched off. It can be imagined that we were in no mood to bow to Coshima but I had no alternative but to give the orders: "*Kioutski*" and "*Keri*" in quick succession; then we marched off.

Nothing further was heard, however, about this effort to enlist voluntary or compulsory broadcasters.

I did not see either of the victims of this outrage again until I returned to 'solitary' but I know that their faces and tongues took many days to heal.

The Japanese had the consummate impertinence to hand us each a slip of paper the next day on which was typed: "Describe your impression of yesterday's happenings."

What they expected us to put, I do not know, for it was made clear that only a short essay was required. We had to be very guarded, but the majority of us took the opportunity of mentioning that we were profoundly shocked by what had taken place. We pointed out that we realised that, as prisoners of war, we were quite defenceless and had to endure what was inflicted upon us, whether we considered it to be just or unjust but that methods of punishment in the East were evidently very different to those to which we had become accustomed in the West.

The Japs only once more tried to get our views broadcast. After an Allied bombing attack, a Japanese interpreter arrived to ask some of our officers if they would broadcast their opinion upon indiscriminate bombing. As no volunteers were forthcoming, the matter was left there but, a day or two later, some officers were detailed to write essays upon their impressions of the bombing. The account of one officer was broadcast without his knowledge or permission. He, as many of us did, had taken the opportunity of essay writing to indulge in sarcasm and to pull the legs of the Japs. They took his gentle witticisms seriously and regarded the reading of the essay as being good propaganda. Probably, it made no difference one way or the other, for any intelligent listener would be unlikely to be affected by an essay read on the wireless which the Japs *claimed* had been written by a British officer.

Tortures and Humiliations

IN the course of this narrative, I tell of specific barbarities of our Japanese masters that were inflicted upon prisoners for specific offences, or imagined offences. Cruel and savage as these were, they were not our main cause for complaint in Rangoon Jail. What was so terrifying was the systematic way in which the Japanese brought into play every device, both physical and mental, to break the spirits of their captives and to make life an absolute misery.

The Japanese are artists in the practice of refined torture but, in Rangoon, they did not confine themselves to the refinements alone. They employed subtle methods but these were supplementary to a main policy of sheer, sustained sadism. They kicked us, they flogged us, they punched us and they starved us.

The Japanese are a thoroughly nasty race and I view with the gravest concern any effort to re-establish them as an important nation in world affairs, no matter from what motives. They will give the appearance of humility, reformation and decency in times of adversity but, as soon as they are in a position to show their true characteristics, they will, once again, manifest themselves as mercenary, uncivilised and arrogant.

This book has no political message but it may be that some of those who read it will be brought to wonder how responsible statesmen can contemplate improving the economic and military position of the Japanese at the present time. I believe that there is the gravest danger that Japan will be allowed to re-habilitate herself in such a way that

73

she will again become a danger to world peace. The Japanese still believe that they are ruled by a descendant of the Gods and that one day the Great Japan will house the whole world under one roof.

The object of the Japanese authorities in Rangoon Jail was two-fold and the position was no different in the other P.O.W. camps, run by the Japanese. They sought to undermine their prisoners physically by methods of slow starvation through the utilisation of diets that resulted in deficiency diseases producing, in many cases, death. Of this, I say more in a subsequent chapter.

Their second object was to produce in the prisoners a state of mental confusion and physical weakness that left them nothing but nervous wrecks. They deliberately set out to turn their prisoners into invalids, incapable of further military or civilian service. This was one of the objects of the solitary confinement to which we were subjected for seventy-seven days after we entered Rangoon Jail. It was the regular treatment for officers and for selected N.C.Os. Some were placed in solitary for as long as a year.

The favourite method of humiliating us adopted by the Japanese, as a matter of routine, was to stand us at attention. Then a Japanese sentry would slap us across the face as hard as he could with both hands. There was no recognition of courage for, if a man stood up to this treatment without wincing, he received further punishment. At times this method was varied by the use of the fist instead of the open hand.

The Japs thought nothing of kicking prisoners on the shin bones with their iron-toed ammunition boots, making scars on the shins, two to four inches long. This was extremely painful treatment and, additionally, the wounds would take weeks to heal. The alternative torture to this was the even more painful and dangerous pastime of kicking the prisoners in the testicles.

One example of the satanic way in which the Japs treated some of our officers was the case of a tall young Sapper lieutenant who was wounded in the chest in North Burma and then taken prisoner. This poor fellow was brought into the jail after marching part of the way and being transported by lorry the rest. He was suffering from a bad attack of beri-beri and his feet, legs, thighs and other parts were very swollen. When I saw him, he had a fresh buckle bruise imprinted on his forehead. He had received this earlier in the day when he had failed to rise to his feet when a Jap sentry entered his cell. It was quite impossible for him to rise without some assistance but the sentry had taken the buckle end of his leather waist-belt and smashed it into the officer's face. The officer had then managed to rise to his feet with the aid of the wall and had received a lashing with the belt.

I told the Jap medical sergeant that this prisoner was in a very bad way indeed and managed, with the consent of Coshima, to have him removed to the prison hospital but, although he put up a brave fight, he became generally oedematous and died.

The buckle ends of these waist-belts were often used on the prisoners as were the butt-ends of rifles and bayonet scabbards and the bayonets themselves. Men were beaten with pieces of split bamboo, which made frightful cuts that took a very long time to heal, and with stout bamboo poles.

One man who did a great deal for his fellow prisoners was Corporal Godwin. He was in Rangoon Jail from May, 1942 and was, in turn, assistant cook in the hospital kitchen, a boot repairer and an assistant in the Japanese Quartermaster's stores. Godwin was a man of robust physique and, perhaps because of this, he was often the target for merciless beatings from the Japanese.

On one occasion, in April 1945, Godwin was taken to the guard room and had his neck, face and hands pummelled by the sentries with their wooden shoes. He stood up to this vicious assault bravely but his face was so cut, bruised and swollen that it was several days before we could ascertain whether his jaw had been fractured or not.

No reason was given to Godwin why he was treated thus but it was, no doubt, connected with the fact that he was sometimes able to smuggle out to other prisoners small quantities of potatoes, vegetables, onions and sugar.

Piper Birse of the Cameronians (Scottish Rifles) was another man whom the Japs treated even worse than they did most of us. He was a short, stocky man but he had a heart like a bullock. He took some terrible bashings from the jailers who did not like his independent, fearless spirit. Several times, he was made to stand to attention, bare-headed in continuous rain or in the broiling sun, for several hours because he failed to bow to the Japanese. Birse was an inspiration to us all. They could not break his spirit, try how they would. When it was all over, he would be seen whistling some Highland melody through his battered lips. Birse too sustained us all by his constant assurance even during the darkest days: "Dinna worry, we'll a' get oot." He almost invited the Jap guards to beat him by his habit of visiting solitary and other British blocks to bring any small extras, that he could steal from the kitchen where he worked, to those prisoners who were in need of them.

All of us experienced this practice of the Japs of making the prisoners stand at attention for hours on end. We were made to stand on our heads in the sun, with our feet resting against a wall for long periods; we were made to stand on one foot with our arms outstretched in the blazing sun on scorching gravel; we were made to stand with our feet against a railing, holding on to it with straightened arms and having to pull ourselves close to the rails whenever a sentry chose to pass and I have seen skeletons of men, suffering from beri-beri, forced to remain for an hour in the sun with a 150 lb. bag of rice on their backs.

Rifleman Hugh McNeill of the Cameronians was once made to stand on his head for five hours during one of the hottest of Burma days. Another time, this soldier was required to hold a heavy plank above his head in the tropical heat for more than an hour.

I was once clouted over the head with a hockey stick, by a sentry nicknamed 'Humpy', when I walked round the barrack rooms with Brigadier Hobson. The 'offence' I had committed was to fail to fix the 'Sanitation Rules' on to the wooden railings with rice paste. The fact that I had made a much better job of the fixing by nailing them on and placing string round the top and bottom to prevent the wind from blowing them away was not counted to me for grace. I can give assurance that a swipe on the top of the skull with a hockey stick is a most unpleasant experience!

Yet perhaps the most terrible punishment of all was not physical. We used to shudder at the very word 'DOKBO', which means, in Japanese, solitary confinement.

There is no doubt that the primary object of this was to cause a mental deterioration and to endeavour to weaken the resistance of the prisoners to Japanese authority. One had to hold on to one's reason like grim death, for the whole procedure could have a devastating effect upon the mind. It is difficult for anyone who has not undergone solitary confinement to realise what it means. I have already said that I was in 'solitary' for seventy-seven days after we moved to Rangoon from Moulmein; now I shall try to describe what it was like. The basic fact was that one was caged up in a dark whitewashed cell for weeks on end and that cell was only 14 feet long by 12 feet broad. The only light came through an iron-barred gate on which was a padlock. That padlock became the symbol of the prisoner's separation from his fellows and could assume tremendous proportions in the imagination. The four factors that militated against sanity were the absence of sunlight, the lack of normal living space, the impossibility of obtaining exercise or of even washing and the fact that one did not have the opportunity of free converse with one's fellows.

From the date of my capture to the end of these seventy-seven days, I was not able to shave or to trim my beard and, as my razor had been stolen by a Jap at Moulmein, I continued without shaving for the rest of my period at Rangoon. My first haircut took place after my release from solitary confinement.

One of the worst features of my spell in 'solitary' was that I had no idea at all how long we were to be kept there. The stay might have been indefinite for all the information that the Japs gave us on the subject. If we had been told that we were to undergo a stated period, we could have braced ourselves up to carry on, in the knowledge that every hour brought our return to more normal conditions nearer. As it was, our endurance had no target. We just had to go on from day to day, hopelessly, living with the nagging fear that we might be in 'solitary' for the rest of our lives.

Yet only one man in Rangoon went mad. This was a tribute to the fortitude and endurance of our fellows. It would not be fair to give the name of the man whose mind broke down, for he was a fine soldier and was even more highly tried than most of us. He had been the victim of a most gruelling exhibition of ju-jitsu only a few days before he broke down. The Japs showed him little sympathy. They just remarked: "*Atama Warri* (head finished)", put him into 'solitary' and left it at that.

The procedure in 'solitary' changed as the days of our imprisonment lengthened and it changed for the worse. Prisoners were kept two or three in the tiny cells, without any bedsteads and had to sit during the day, side by side, without speaking, with their backs leaning against the walls. They were not allowed to move except to collect their meals or to visit the *benjo* (sanitary pail) in the cell.

There were times too when some of the occupants of 'solitary' fared very badly indeed at meals, especially if they were among the last to be served. They would receive less than the starvation diet upon which the rest of us were expected to live. They would receive either a very small rice ration without any *dahl* (a small lentil-like bean) or just a little meat and vegetables.

I appealed to the medical sergeant many times to allow officers to purchase from their allowances such extras for the sick in solitary as we could afford. For a time this was allowed but it was later stopped without any reason being given. Sometimes too, the sentries would not allow the officers to have any extras sent over from the kitchen. They would either tell the Chinese prisoners who delivered the meals to take these or would put them down the open latrine pit outside the block.

Some of the prisoners in 'solitary' never had any proper mess tins or plates, neither were there any spoons or forks. Mess tins were made out of corrugated iron in the shape of small rectangular trays, at the order of the Japs, by some of the B.O.R. prisoners. Two hundred were ordered to be made on one occasion and each new prisoner received two.

The cell floors in 'solitary' were never washed, because of the scarcity of water there. During the time that I was in, we had great difficulty in getting a bath, in the sticky tropical conditions, once a week for the same reason.

Spoons we did have, made out of pieces of bamboo but there were no drinking mugs. We just had to have a drink out of the mess tin after we had finished eating from it.

Sometimes the Japs would take away the prisoners' blankets and coverings and at other times would put us on a water diet for several days. Brigadier Hobson, when he was in 'solitary' was put on a water diet for ten days by Coshima.

Benjo tins had to be emptied by each officer at this time into a common stinking latrine. This was only done once a day and it was not very pleasant in the tropics to have tins containing excreta and urine in the cell with one all day.

During the last year of our imprisonment, prisoners in 'solitary' were taken out into the yard and taught Japanese drill and made to do P.T. This was somewhat fatiguing for men in the condition we were in, but it did at least make a break in the soul-destroying routine.

The day's timetable was very much the same as in the other compounds, except that we were visited by the Nip N.C.Os. and did not have to go on parade. They came round at any time from eight to nine thirty. We were then allowed out briefly to empty our *benjo* tins and to have a wash. Then we were locked in our cells again and, after we had tidied them, our breakfast was brought. From ten o'clock onwards, we did ten to twenty minutes P.T. by walking round our cells close to the wall over a hundred times. The midday meal was brought sometime after one o'clock and the evening meal about six. Apart from another short period of P.T. before supper we had nothing to do all day except look around us and think, unless we had been able to get hold of a book through the kindness of B.O.Rs. who had been out on working parties.

The cells in 'solitary' were cockroach-ridden and infected by lice and bed-bugs. I formed the habit of trying to while away the time by recalling to my mind passages of poetry memorised in my school days. The lines:

> "Stone walls do not a prison make,
> Nor iron bars a cage.
> Minds innocent and quiet take
> That for a hermitage."

would haunt me. They would keep running through my mind and I could not stop thinking about them for hours at a time.

Again in the evenings those familiar lines of Newboult's *Vitai Lampada* would come crowding back; as the evening sun shone into my 'solitary' cell:

> "There's a breathless hush in the close tonight,
>   Ten to make and the match to win
>   A bumping pitch and a blinding light
>   An hour to play and the last man in."

But there was no pitch—only the breathless hush of the solitary cells—but the match was won on the morning of 29th August, 1945, many miles away from Rangoon.

Time and time again, I tried to write out the words of Kipling's *If*. I still have one of my efforts with many words altered and re-inserted among the blank spaces. I was always stumped by the last four lines of the first stanza—the lines beginning:

> "If you can wait and not be tired of waiting,
>   Or being lied about, don't deal in lies . . ."

No doubt the psychiatrists would have an explanation of my failure in this respect!

Doctoring under Difficulties

WHEN I emerged into the ordinary prison routine after my seventy-seven days in 'solitary', one thing was quite clear to me. In spite of Coshima's boast that the Japanese had 'plenty of good doctors', it was evident that they had 'no good doctors' to spare for the prisoners of war in Rangoon Jail. The only provision that the Japanese made for medical attention for our men was an occasional visit to the jail from a junior medical officer from the hospital in Rangoon. The prison hospitals and sick bays were serviced by N.C.Os., who were not even trained medical orderlies in the Japanese Medical Corps. I did what I could to organise a prison medical service, as was my duty as the Senior Medical Officer in Rangoon Jail.

In addition to McLeod and myself, there were a number of other doctors in the jail. We did not have poor Kilgour with us long, for he died while we were in 'solitary'. Incidentally his death provided the only opportunity for my leaving the confines of the jail during the whole period of my imprisonment. I was hurriedly called out of the Punishment Cells one August afternoon, informed that Captain Kilgour had died of dysentery (although I do not think that there is much doubt that he died of beri-beri), told that I was to take the funeral service and transported with the loathsome Coshima to the English cemetery at Rangoon. On this occasion, the Japanese sent a wreath, a practice they soon discontinued, and I read a short service over the body of my colleague.

The other doctors in the jail, although none of them were

My dear Doktor!

I want to know about the Jungle Sore and I.A.T. concerning to officers or soldiers who has Jungle Sore and I. A. T.; Answer the following questions.
<u>Please</u>

A) Name and Age.
B) The body Weight before the War.
C) When began the Decease?
D) Where and why? (for Example, in Jungle, in the house,
   thrust through (pierce) by the branches of trees, etc.)
E) Symptoms (The Detail of the Decease)

The Army Surgeon
Dr. Ikegami.

Letter received by the Author from Japanese Medical Officer in Rangoon Jail.

in our compound, were Captain Brahmanath Sudan of the Burma Army Medical Corps and the following officers of the Indian Medical Service: Captain Ahmed, Captain Dwgaprarod Rao, Lieutenant Alexander K. Thomas and Lieutenant Pillai. Later we were joined, early in 1944, by Major Raymond Ramsay of the R.A.M.C., who did really splendid work, coming, as he did, at a time when the rest of us were ill and exhausted.

The general layout of Rangoon Jail, where I had to organise an improvised medical service, can be understood from the plan inserted in this book. The various blocks are numbered. The central Water Tower was, in many ways, the hub of the whole organisation, for it was used as the Q.M. store and as a water-drawing point as well as being the location of the bean-germinating plant that I established and having a side passage that became our 'operating theatre'. The Tower derived its name from the fact that it had, in its centre, a deep well that was used in the all too frequent times of emergency when the main prison supply, which came from Mingaladon and beyond, failed.

The blocks were of uniform construction. Each had a ground floor of cement and an upper floor of wood, which was reached by cement steps at both ends. These blocks were reputed to be earthquake-proof and they were certainly able to stand up to the bombing that took place on two or three occasions towards the end of our imprisonment. On each floor were five rooms with five long, barred windows on each side. These windows had no glass and did permit a certain amount of breeze and fresh air to enter the rooms day and night. The maximum authorised capacity of each room, during the days of British rule in Burma, was twenty-eight. In each block, two of the upstairs rooms were allotted to officers, who slept twenty-six in a room. The other rooms were occupied by other ranks, who lived, in the first year or so, forty or forty-four to a room. The end room downstairs was used as a hospital and M.I. Room and four orderlies slept in a bunk that was at the end of the verandah that ran round the block.

I was in No. 3 Block and our conditions of accommodation improved somewhat when, early in 1944, the Japs, as an administrative measure, decided to close our hospital and transfer all the patients to three rooms in No. 6 Block, which housed American and colonial prisoners. Then Brigadier Hobson was able to persuade the Japs to keep the numbers in all rooms in No. 3 Block to a maximum of thirty-two.

In the compound outside No. 3 Block were two kitchens which we constructed from corrugated iron sheets. Brick and mud, with a little cement, formed the base for the vats in which the eternal rice was cooked. There was an open fireplace of bricks in one of the shacks and a home-made oven in the other, that was used for cooking food, apart from rice.

In the compound also was a cement trough, about thirty feet long, three feet broad and three feet deep. It had several taps at one end. This trough was used as a bath and, when the water was coming through from Mingaladon, it served the purpose satisfactorily. Towards the end, however, it suffered from the bombing and leaked very badly indeed.

At the other end of the compound from the bath was a very much less satisfactory feature of the jail. Here were the latrines and the dug urinal. The latrines were filthy beyond description and, consequently, a breeding ground for all sorts of infections. We did not have enough latrine tins, and those we did have leaked badly. The floor of the latrines was always wet from the soakage of these tins and gave off an abominable and revolting smell, in spite of the fact that our sanitary squad bravely washed it twice a day. Lids were made for the tins by the latrine staff out of corrugated iron, which abated the fly nuisance somewhat in that particular place. The Japs were able to grasp the idea that flies were a bad thing in the compound, but that is about all they were able to grasp in this connection. They were always shouting to us to kill flies about the block but they did not think there was anything untoward in the procedure they enforced, whereby the contents of the latrine tins were taken each day and dumped in an enormous open shell hole. When the shell hole became full, the excreta was taken to the vegetable gardens and hurriedly covered over with an inch or two of dirt or earth. The shell hole and the gardens became a breeding place for millions of flies.

I suggested to the Japs early on that they should allow us to dig Otway's Pits, to minimise the fly nuisance in the jail. They refused to sanction this plan. Instead, the vegetable preparation shed and the rice store were established in the gardens.

No praise can be too high for the sanitary squad in No. 3 Block. They worked ceaselessly and cheerfully at their thankless and filthy task. In addition to their responsibility for their own block, they later had to carry out latrine duties for the prisoners in 'solitary' as well, a considerable additional responsibility when the numbers there were over a hundred. This small band of men were then dealing with disposal for some four hundred men, many of them suffering from dysentery, beri-beri and other diseases that made an unpleasant task even more loathsome. They had, of course, no masks and no proper disinfectants.

Conditions were worst during the monsoons. The surface of the compounds was 'muttie' and drainage was nonexistent. We had to walk out in bare feet through squelching, sticky mud, water and latrine washings to perform our natural functions, both by day and by night. Then we had to return to our quarters and, at night, get back into bed.

There was nothing on which to wipe or dry the feet. The bed coverings became masses of the infectious germs of intestinal diseases.

During the rains, there was not a dry room or verandah in the blocks. The corrugated iron roofs leaked as a result of the bombings and ack-ack shelling of 1941. I will admit that the position here was not improved by the fact that some of our men, when they went up to the roofs to try to repair them, were inclined to take wooden beams, rafters and floor boards to add to our scant fuel supply!

When I came out of 'solitary', I found that the hospital of No. 3 Block was being run by Company-Sergeant Major Finnerty of the Royal Inniskilling Fusiliers. This admirable Warrant Officer entered Rangoon Jail in April, 1942 and he took considerable risks to maintain the morale of all ranks. As soon as he arrived at the jail, in spite of the fact that he was suffering from the effects of severe wounds, he assumed full responsibility for organising the British block, for feeding the troops and for running the hospital, in spite of the greatest difficulties and obstruction he encountered from the Japanese.

When all the officers were in 'solitary', Finnerty succeeded in maintaining contact with us, getting extra quantities of food smuggled into the solitary cells and transmitting news by signal (he was an expert signaller), at considerable personal risk. Later, he took on responsibility for pay and for arranging the working parties, as well as being in charge of all the internal economy of the block.

When I assumed responsibility for the medical services in No. 3 Block from Finnerty, who had done magnificently, with no specialised training or experience, I was appalled by the difficulties with which I was faced. Our men accepted my authority willingly and gladly, but the fact had to be faced that any Japanese private was able to countermand my orders not only in regard to Service discipline but also in matters of medical treatment. I had, therefore, to move with the greatest possible caution.

We called one room in the block a 'hospital' but it was a strange hospital indeed. There were virtually no dressings, no drugs and no instruments available and it was impossible to order proper diets for prisoners suffering from deficiency diseases, for the Japs would not allow us to have the food, necessary to deal with these conditions. The 'hospital' was really no better than just a room in which were congregated those men who were ill, some of them dying.

I do not believe that it is possible for anybody who was not with us to appreciate fully the conditions under which men were ill or became ill. We were living crowded together in wretched conditions; we existed in mud and filth throughout the hot and humid monsoon season for six months of the year; we roasted on gravel and cement in the broiling sun; we wore the scantiest of clothing, mainly *fundoshis*; we had no headgear and most of the men, except for a few who had wooden sandals, had to go about barefooted. We were ill-treated and had no food suitable for Europeans. There was very little water available for washing or cooking and a really cold drink was a luxury that we never experienced. There was no electric light, no fans or punkahs. In spite of all this, the B.O.Rs. were expected to march on the hot tarmac roads and visit all parts of Rangoon as working parties. The squalor, stink and misery of such conditions, depressing and humiliating, took a heavy toll and the plight of the sick and suffering cannot adequately be described by any words that are at my command.

The only difference between the hospital and the other rooms in the block was that the patients did not have to go on working parties and were not expected to attend the morning and evening roll-call parades. Some of the patients were given old, condemned, mosquito nets but most were without any nets at all. The Japanese insisted that all cases of colic and dysentery wore half blankets around their waists in bed. There were no pillows for the patients, although I asked the Japanese for these several times. In the hospital, the latrines were within the room and consisted of old .303 ammunition boxes. These were only emptied and washed morning and evening and this task was performed by the hospital orderlies. These men had no gloves or special overalls nor had they any proper equipment. They just had to utilise small pieces of cloth, chunks of dry grass or brushes they were able to make out of bamboo and odd bits of sacking.

The ordinary prisoners never received any toilet paper but the Japanese medical N.C.O. would sometimes bring in small issues of cut-up Japanese books for use by the diarrhoea cases.

Bedpans were unknown in the jail and there was only one proper commode for the whole hospital. The volunteer nursing orderlies, who were under a sergeant, had to help the beri-beri patients across the room to visit the ammunition tins. Some of these patients were passing from twelve to twenty stools every twenty-four hours so the orderlies were kept pretty busy on this work alone.

The drug position was quite impossible. At no time did we have sufficient of any drug and many of those that were issued were quite inefficacious. Even with quite simple drugs, the Japanese refused to issue them to us in sufficient quantities. If I said, for example, that a patient required ten grains of aspirin, thrice daily, the Nips would only issue sufficient for him to have five grains, twice daily. At other times, they would simply say that no aspirin was available. It was interesting to note that all the aspirin issued was of well-known British proprietary brands—obviously looted from civilian chemists' shops in Rangoon at the time of the occupation.

The same applied to dressings. When we got them, which was not often, they were either captured British or Indian Army supplies or had been stolen from the stores in Rangoon.

To obtain dusting powder, we were given small quantities of poor quality boric powder, starch and talcum and told to mix these together. Very occasionally, we were issued with a small dredger of dusting powder manufactured by Messrs. Boots of Nottingham.

No respectable store, even in the poorest districts of Great Britain, would stock the kind of medicines that the Japanese issued to us. The quinine tablets we obtained were badly coated and packed in such a way that most of their value was destroyed by the damp of the climate of Burma. Calomel was made up into five-grain tablets and we had to cut these up before we could use them for treatment. That sounds easy enough but it was a bit of a trial when no proper cutting instrument was available. Once or twice, we were allowed some so-called sulphona-mide tablets for pneumonia patients. They were not very effective. It took a major crisis to persuade the Nips to release sedative tablets and we were not much better off when they did. When used for sleep-producing purposes they seemed to have little effect.

One difficulty that arose for which we could not fairly blame the Japs was that they were inclined to talk of grammes whereas we talked of grains. As there are 15 grains in a gramme, it was essential to get this matter clear before trying treatment in particular cases.

Gauze was an ever-present problem. We were given practically none and had to make do with pieces of muslin or bandage cloth and even, on some occasions, with pieces of khaki. We would cut these materials up into small pieces and soak them in boiling water in a mess tin or chipped enamel bowl. The cotton wool was dirty off-white in colour and was almost non-absorbent. We had to soak this in hot water and wring it out before we could use it as swabs. That exhausted the uses to which we were able to put hot water in our practice of medicine for we had very little hot water available. It was impossible to waste it washing bandages. These we cleaned in cold water and we washed them again and again, until they became absolutely useless.

Hydrogen sulphide was issued for a time for the treatment of ringworm. Iodine was extremely scarce and had no strength, except on the rare occasions when we were fortunate enough to be issued with our own B.P. preparations. We were very fortunate in one respect. There were large quantities of copper sulphate lying about the jail. Where it had come from originally, I was never able to find out, but it was invaluable in the treatment of sores, especially that variety known in the East as 'jungle-sores'. We used it in solutions of differing strengths and it proved very effective.

Later the Japs maintained that better results would be obtained by using a dilute cresol solution and pure carbolic acid. A Japanese medical orderly gave a demonstration of this treatment and then passed over the responsibility of administering it to a Chinese prisoner whose normal employment was cleaning up the wards! I shudder even now when I think of this episode. The first few victims had their sores washed with a small swab, soaked in the cresol solution, to clear any sloughs or membrane and then had the sores washed with pure carbolic. The result was an influx of patients into Ramsay's hospital in No. 6 Block suffering from pure carbolic acid burns. I took a stand on this matter and refused to allow any more of our men to attend for this treatment. We were then allowed to carry through a modified treatment in our own block M.I. room and the results were very satisfactory because we took care to dry off all traces of carbolic acid from the ulcer bed and contented ourselves with dressing the sores twice a day instead of applying the acid twice a day.

Many of these 'jungle-sores' were of a diphtheroid type and, if dealt with rather vigorously to begin with, healed fairly rapidly. If, however, they were left until infection had undermined the skin edges, treatment was a long and painful process.

The infection of 'jungle-sores' that afflicted our block was, almost certainly, transmitted through the Chinese Block. Several months prior to the appearance of the sores in No. 3 Block, I was called over to the Chinese Block by one of the Nip N.C.Os. and asked for my opinion on two cases of 'jungle-sores'. At that time I had no experience of this condition and I suggested that they might take scrapings, culture them and carry out a microscopic examination to see what was the predominating infection. They took samples away with them but I never heard the result of the examination.

My theory is that the sores arrived at our block from No. 6 Block hospital, after having been transmitted there from the Chinese Block. It was certainly not until we received prisoners from No. 6 Block hospital and some of our own sick had returned from there that the trouble arose. I formed the opinion that they were, in some cases, infected by diphtheroids, because before Major Ramsay took over medical charge of No. 6 Block, I had found there two cases of clinical faucial diphtheria.

One of these cases was a tailor and he was probably responsible for droplet infection. He did not report sick until he developed typical post-diphtheritic paralysis, paralysis of accommodation, regurgitation of fluids through his nose, peripheral neuritis of the hands and legs and a sore throat. He died a short time afterwards with cardiac involvement. He might have lived if we had been given the antitoxin for which we asked.

To Brig. Gen Hobson
   through Capt. B.N. Sudan BAMC   March 4, '44

Dear Sir,
          I beg to inform you that for more
than 6 months our sickmen, with the permission
of the Japanese, have been placed under the medical
care of four British medical officers. Capts. Sudan,
Pillay, Thomas & Rau, all Indian officers of
the British Army. Among them Capt. B.N. Sudan's
services have been especially invaluable to us. During
this period we have not a single death and three
of our soldiers were virtually snatched away from
the very jaws of death – all through the effort of
that good officer. In consideration of the difficult
difficulties imposed upon by the Japanese and the
regretable lack of medical facilities at present,
he has certainly done a great deal. It would
indeed be ungrateful on my part not to acknowledge
the very creditable services he has rendered to us. It
is therefore, only just for me to bring his excellent
services to the notice of the most senior British
officer here and to express our appreciations and
thanks thereby.
          I will be ready and be only too glad to bear
testimony to the above statement when called upon to
do so at any time after the war if I am lucky enough
to survive it.
          I beg to remain, Respectfully yours,
                              Lt. Gen. Chi Chiang

Letter from General Chi to Brigadier Hobson

Major McLeod from Ontario, Canada, with one of his patients, Cpl. J. Usher, whose leg he successfully amputated without an anaesthetic

The other case was wise enough to report his symptoms very much earlier and we arrested further progress of the disease by the use of strong carbolic, locally to the fauces, and carbolic gargles.

Ointments were also in short supply. Vaseline, to which the Nip orderlies used to add carbolic acid or boric powder, was issued from time to time, but more often we had to make do with some dreadful Japanese zinc ointment.

At first, I had no instruments at all. Then Gavin, one of our nursing orderlies, had the bright idea of making for me a scalpel out of a much used safety-razor blade. That he fixed into a short piece of wood about five inches long and, with it, I was able to make small, superficial incisions into boils and abscesses.

On three occasions, I did more than this. I used the home-made scalpel for minor operations. I took a bullet out of the back of a soldier; I removed a fragment of shell from the base of an American airman's little finger; and I took another fragment from a second soldier's thigh muscle. In each case, the metal had been in for months and the wound had healed by primary intention, then it either started to give pain and discharge or lit up with infection.

My first pair of forceps was made from a piece of hammered-out zinc sheet but it was not a success. The blade gave, if much pressure was exercised. Some of the men on working parties then managed to 'win' a pair of artery forceps for me, when they were out. These were extremely useful and it was a heartrending experience one morning to find them broken because somebody had used them for an unauthorised purpose. A small thing like that can be such a tragedy in the circumstances in which we found ourselves.

We were never free of the Japs in the hospitals. They would walk round at any hour of the day and tell us how to treat our patients. Their panacea for diarrhoea and beri-beri cases was charcoal and rice-water. Of course, we took

7

no notice of their advice, except to warn the patients to reply, when they were asked what they were receiving: "Charcoal and rice-water".

There was no hospital clothing for the patients. They had to sleep and lie in what scanty clothing they possessed and to spend their time between soiled blankets. The splendid untrained men who acted as hospital orderlies did all that they could—more than could reasonably be expected. They worked staggering hours, washing, when we had many patients with various diseases causing diarrhoea, in an almost hopeless race to prevent the patients from having to lie in their own excreta, day after day.

One thing the Japanese were very keen about was that we should vaccinate and inoculate against plague, cholera and typhoid. Whenever they had vaccine lymph or vaccines, they worried us to carry through a full-scale inoculation. This precaution, as understood by the Japanese, however, served little purpose.

When we first started to vaccinate and inoculate the prisoners, we tried to carry through the procedure in the manner to which we had been accustomed. We used a freshly-sterilised needle for each case. The Japs, however, took very serious exception to this as they said it took much too long. They demanded that we carried out inoculations continuously with one needle. We were ordered to make no effort to sterilise the needle between insertions and were only allowed to stop, when the syringe of 10 or 20 c.c. capacity became empty. On one occasion, we were ordered to carry out, at one session, a small-pox vaccination and inoculations against plague and cholera. All the equipment we were allowed was two needles, two syringes and a vaccination scarifier. More than five hundred men passed through our hands during this venture. The method we adopted was as follows:

The left arm was daubed with a blob of cotton wool

soaked in iodine, on a thin bamboo stick. Both the cotton wool and the iodine were of the usual inferior quality. A dose of cholera vaccine was injected, then the arm was swabbed again with more iodine. The right arm was then washed with cotton wool, through which some soapy water had been squeezed. The arm, when dry, was then scarified and vaccine lymph applied. Then we swabbed the breast region with iodine and injected plague vaccine with another syringe and needle. After being swabbed, each man was told not to wash the vaccine off the vaccinated arm.

I recommended the men to have these vaccinations and inoculations, in spite of the fact that the conditions were so bad. I told them that I was having them myself but conceded that no man need have them, if he preferred not to do so. They all agreed to undergo the ordeal and we had the amazing sequel that, of five hundred officers and men who underwent the treatment, only one sergeant developed a small cutaneous abscess. Ramsay helped me with this mass inoculation and he and I spent several unhappy days and nights after the performance, awaiting the consequences that we felt certain would follow.

If this procedure had been carried through with due precautions, it would have meant many days, work, but the Japs made us get through it in hours. One difficulty was that we never knew what products we were using or the strengths or dosages we were injecting. I am certain, however, that the dosages must have been very weak, for it was my practice to give myself a double injection each time, as a control, and I never suffered any ill effects.

Only once during the whole of our stay in jail did we have a visit from a Japanese dentist. He was a private soldier but was a qualified, and seemed to be a competent, dentist. He had with him a captured British Dental Roll and with the aid of two per cent Novocaine and a dental syringe, he performed a few extractions.

One short visit from a dentist in nearly three years, however, made little impression upon the dental problem with which we were faced. I, therefore, turned myself into a dentist. The Japs allowed us to borrow the old pattern dental case that was in the possession of Captain Sudan of the Burma Army Medical Corps, when he was captured, and I used this. Quite apart from teeth that required extraction through normal decay, I had dozens of cases in which I had to extract wisdom teeth. The majority of our prisoners were men under twenty-six years of age and, probably because of the rice diet and the lack of conservative treatment, many of them began erupting or half-erupting their wisdom teeth. I do not think that many men would have had their teeth pulled out by me, if they had not been suffering considerable pain. I had no anaesthetics to give them and was only able to use a piece of wood as a prop, instead of a gag. A man who consents to have a wisdom tooth extracted, with septic roots from a bed of pus, in these circumstances, must be pretty desperate. As it was, so great did my reputation as a dentist grow, that even the Japanese sentries asked me to extract their teeth in a similar fashion. I did not mind causing them a bit of pain!

Men Died who should have Lived

THE object of this book is, most certainly, not to draw attention to the misfortunes and ill health I suffered personally in Rangoon Jail. I only want to note in passing that I was an ill man, most of the time, and that I should have died, had it not been for the kindly way in which my companions stood by me and did what they could to ease my lot. The life I was forced to lead was probably for me a greater strain than it was for most of my fellow prisoners, because, almost without exception, they were young men, whereas I was in the fifties. I contracted the deficiency diseases one by one and they took their toll. Additionally, my eyesight got progressively worse and I lived in a state of purblindness. Were it not that Captain Colgan gave me his spare pair of glasses, which just enabled me to read and discern letters and figures, my usefulness as a medical officer would have been very small. As it was, apart from the times when I was too weak and ill to get about, I was privileged to act in my professional capacity throughout the long months when men lay desperately ill and dying around me.

My position was one of particular responsibility. I was, as a full Colonel, not only the senior R.A.M.C. officer in the jail, but also the senior British regular officer there. Brigadier Hobson held a higher rank but he was the holder of an emergency commission and his rank had been given to him in the special circumstances of his acting as a liaison officer with the Chinese forces. He had no experience of routine soldiering and he had not spent very much time with officers and men of the Army previously. I say this with no desire to disparage a man who rose to the emergency, in which he found himself, magnificently, but his position led him to lean the more heavily upon regular officers and it is a tribute to his tact and sense of responsibility that he was able to do so without arousing either resentment or friction. Hobson had travelled widely in the East as a representative of tobacco companies and the experience, thus gained, was of the greatest use to us in our efforts to understand the psychology of the Japanese and what was likely to be their reactions to particular events. He was a tall, stoutish man of early middle-age and had very little hair. He put my one pack of cards to good use for he was a splendid bridge player and one of the most inscrutable holders of cards I have ever met. He and I agreed, soon after we met, that the best way to wring concessions out of the Japanese was to be complete hypocrites.

My hypocrisy took the form of playing upon the fact that the Japanese had more respect for old men than they had for young ones. I was half-blind and I pretended to be half-deaf, and sometimes half-daft, as well. My attacks of beri-beri enabled me to give the impression quite easily that I was a venerable figure indeed and this pose was assisted by my grizzled, grey beard. We got few enough drugs and dressings but many of those we did get were obtained, because the Japs traditionally had acquired the habit of giving countenance to the importunities of their elders. My old age, too, was largely responsible for the fact that I was able to persuade the Japs to allow the medical treatment of prisoners to pass progressively into the hands of my colleagues and myself. Perhaps my greatest triumph in this direction, though, was when, after persistent solicitation, the Nips allowed me to classify our prisoners into four categories: Cripples, No-duty men, Light-duty men and Full-duty men.

The intermediate category of Light-duty men was of particular value, for it enabled us to lift many men, whom we would not have been allowed to place in the No-duty class, out of the depths of despair. Men, who were given this classification, were employed as brushmakers, making the rough sweepers' bamboo brushes, as hammerers of mess-tins out of corrugated zinc, and on peeling vegetables, sorting rice and doing general fatigues. Principally, however, they were drafted to the strange task of candlemaking.

The Japanese were inclined to encourage candlemaking, for candles were greatly in demand by the Rangoon civilian population and they were able to charge inflated prices for them. The indefatigable C.S.M. Finnerty was placed in charge of this work and it consisted of cutting out paper cartons, filling them with melted tallow and packing them into wicker baskets. The numbers employed on this work varied between twenty and forty and they were always having their attention drawn to the exploits of some Japanese women who were similarly employed in Rangoon. These women were turning out fifteen hundred candles a day. Our men, with a little experience, soon passed this mark and eventually were turning out in the region of eight thousand candles a day. This scheme continued successfully for a time but, as the War progressed, the Japs found it increasingly difficult to get supplies of tallow, output went down, days of idleness were frequent and finally the whole organisation broke down in February or March, 1945.

The diseases which we were called upon to treat were many and varied, but it is a most extraordinary thing that we had no single case of sunstroke or heat exhaustion amongst the British and American prisoners. This was really remarkable in view of the fact that the incidence of these conditions has always been fairly high amongst European troops in the tropics. I can offer no adequate explanation of this phenomenon but my view is that we were free because we lacked what had previously been considered to be proper headdress, footwear and protective clothing and, thus, readier evaporation from the body was permitted. This theory is borne out to some extent by the additional fact that none of our men suffered from prickly heat, which was epidemic amongst British troops serving actively in Burma.

I believe that this is a matter that would repay considerable investigation by medical scientists, for it may well be that the European approach to the problem of living in the tropics is a wrong one. Exposure of the body may well be a more effective answer than protection of the body. A pointer is given by the fact that, as recently as my early days in India, it was considered suicidal for a European to venture out into the sun without a topee on his head. The war taught us that this view was merely a fetish and tens of thousands of British troops served in South-East Asia, without ever seeing, let alone wearing, a topee.

We had an enormous number of cases of scabies and ringworm of the body and the close association of ringworm and beri-beri was marked.

We had some cases of body lice but fortunately they were not in evidence frequently. On the other hand, we were never free of bed-bugs. I do not think that there was a single man in the jail who was not badly bitten at some time or another. Bed-bugs are loathsome, irritating creatures with a most horrible smell and their bites give rise to a good deal of discomfort. They were obviously well-established in Rangoon Jail long before we got there, and after a time one got used to them.

Malaria and dengue fevers were fairly common in their seasonable incidence each year. Many of the malaria cases were relapses, who had not received adequate quinine or atebrin treatment initially. Fortunately, we were never overwhelmed by malaria cases and we were able to effect cures in the great majority of instances. In doing this, we were assisted by men of the working parties who would smuggle effective quinine tablets into the jail. If we had had to rely upon the Japanese quinine tablets, about which I have already written, the more serious cases would have presented a difficult problem indeed. We did not see any mepacrine. Dengue fever was a good deal more troublesome for, apart from the seasonable incidence, cases occurred all the year round. All we had to prescribe were aspirin tablets and I must admit that these were not very effective in serious cases. Sometimes we varied the treatment a little by giving the Japanese creosote capsules, when there appeared to be chest symptoms, but these served little purpose, except to give the patient the assurance and mental satisfaction that he was receiving the best possible treatment.

During the rainy seasons, we had a few cases of pneumotoxaemia. These were extremely difficult to diagnose, unless one kept the possibility of their occurrence before one. I devised a formula which I used to repeat to myself every morning before my sick parade. It ran thus: "Apart from the commonest cases of plague, cholera and typhus, when are we going to meet with smallpox, diphtheria or aberrant pneumonic infection?"

Smallpox appeared in due course. I had been expecting it for some time in view of our close proximity to the Chinese prisoners of war and of the filthy conditions under which our men had to perform coolie labour in Rangoon, coming into contact with natives suffering from all manner of diseases, including leprosy, elephantiasis and every kind of skin trouble. The infection did not reach us from the Chinese block, for, strangely enough, they did not have a single case of smallpox there.

Smallpox was contracted by two officers. I was called to No. 6 Block hospital one afternoon to see the first case. I was quite familiar with the disease, for I had attended a good many Indians with smallpox in pre-war days. I realised what was wrong, while I was still a good distance away from the officer. I could see the distribution of the vesicles on his face and on the extensor aspects of his wrists and hands. I questioned him and found out that he had missed being vaccinated when his unit was done at Bangalore, as he had been away from the camp at the time. I turned to Ramsay and said: "I am afraid that the diagnosis is obvious."

We did what we could, but he died within a few days. A short time afterwards, the second officer became ill, but he had a mild attack, for he, fortunately, did bear the marks of previous vaccination. He had been in close contact with the man who died and the comparative lightness of his attack could only be attributed to vaccination.

When we reported to the Japs that we had smallpox cases in the jail, they went into a panic and were completely co-operative in acceding to our suggestion that everybody should be re-vaccinated immediately. This speedy action of ours prevented what would almost certainly have been a severe epidemic. In our No. 3 Block alone, there were seven prisoners whose re-vaccination was successful, which meant that they were susceptible to smallpox.

We had lost our hospital in No. 3 Block by the time the first case of cholera occurred amongst us. Once a white man contracted cholera in the conditions under which we were living, it was an almost hopeless undertaking to give him any treatment. Our task was to make his dying hours as comfortable as possible and to move with the utmost speed to prevent an epidemic. If cholera had obtained a substantial hold in Rangoon Jail, it would have eliminated the prisoners, like straw before a prairie fire. It would have been little compensation that it would also have eliminated the Japs!

Cholera started this way. A private soldier came back from Rangoon with his working party one evening and complained that he had a terrible and unnatural hunger. He ate his own supper of rice, meat and vegetables and two of his comrades gave him part of their rations also. That night, he began to suffer severe abdominal pain and attacks of acute diarrhoea. In the early morning, he soiled his own blankets, the floor and the blankets of two other men in an effort to get to the latrines. His companions put his bed out on the verandah and it was there that I was called to see him. I was struck immediately by the dehydrated appearance of the man; he looked as though all the water had been drained out of his body. His eyes were sunken, he had a poor pulse, there were frequent spasms of abdominal colic and his cheeks had a somewhat cyanosed appearance. I asked him if he had swallowed anything, while he was out of the jail, but he denied having done so. As he reported the heavy meal he had taken the previous night, I took his statement at its face value.

I had the man removed over to the No. 6 Block hospital, and told them there that the patient was rather collapsed and that he was suffering from some type of choleraic diarrhoea, that would require very careful watching. In the hospital, he was given a bunk in the middle of the ward amongst the beri-beri patients.

Next morning, when I went over to No. 6 Block, I found that several men around him were suffering from severe abdominal cramp. They were all vomiting and passing involuntary liquid stools, that were splashing on the floor underneath their beds.

We immediately informed the Japs that cholera had broken out and we were allowed to isolate the cases in a separate room. I told Major Ramsay to clear the ward where the cases had been, for three or four days, and we burnt the bamboo platforms and disinfected the room, as best we could, with cresol and chloride of lime.

We were hopelessly equipped to deal with the outbreak. There were no anti-cholera outfits available, we had no protective clothing, no gloves, no rubber Wellington boots for the medical staff or the orderlies. In fighting cholera, it is essential to have oils, drugs, intravenous saline-infusion apparatus and sodium chloride tablets. We had none of these.

I remembered that the Red Cross at Geneva would always supply material, in time of war, to prevent epidemics. I, therefore, wrote an appeal to the Commandant, asking him whether it would be possible for the Japanese military headquarters at Rangoon to broadcast an appeal to the nearest neutral representative, or even to India, and ask that twenty complete cholera outfits should be forwarded to Rangoon Jail by air, as there was the gravest danger that the number of American and British prisoners in the jail would be decimated through a cholera epidemic. I considered that there was at least a faint hope that my appeal would be given favourable consideration, for a new Commandant had replaced Coshima by this time. He came down to No. 3 Block the next morning and told us that his superiors had refused to countenance any such appeal. He had the grace to say that he regretted this—as well he might, for he and his men were in as grave danger as we were.

Once we had isolated the cases and the contacts, there was little that we could do except hope for the best. We were extremely fortunate, for no further case occurred outside that limited circle, except for one orderly, a Cameronian who volunteered for duty with the first patient and who contracted the disease a couple of days later and died.

The epidemic ran its course in fourteen days. We lost

eight to ten men and their corpses were burnt inside the jail walls, as soon as they died. Outside working parties were suspended for a period.

After the original case died, Private Goldstone reported to me that he had seen this man drinking a mess-tin full of water from a disused well in a compound where they were working!

We had comparatively few cases of dysentery in Rangoon Jail although, to begin with, many cases of camp diarrhoea and beri-beri were so diagnosed. Large numbers of men suffered from lob-worms and thread-worms but I never saw a case of tape-worm. We managed to get on top of these conditions eventually, to some extent, by the purchase of onions and garlic, both of which have strong anti-worm properties.

Our great scourge, however, was beri-beri and a large proportion of the thirty-three per cent of our men who died were finished off by this condition. As the average person at home is not familiar with beri-beri, I shall say something about the disease, before I go on to tell of the measures we adopted to deal with it. Particularly, I would point out that most of the deaths from this cause were unnecessary, for, if the Japs had fed us properly, the incidence of the disease would have been negligible.

Beri-beri is a deficiency disease and the Japanese were perfectly familiar with the causes of it. My friend, W. R. Aykroyd, writing in *Vitamins and Other Dietary Essentials*, published by Heinemann in 1933, records: "In 1878, beri-beri occurred in the Japanese Navy to the extent of putting 300 out of every thousand men on the sick list; in 1888 it had practically ceased to be of importance to the naval medical officers. The decade had seen no far-reaching improvement in sanitation, no essential alterations in the routine of a Japanese man-of-war, but, in the interval, Admiral Takaki had changed the rations. Instead of polished rice with a little fish and vegetables, the Japanese sailors were given wheat, barley, beans, milk, meat and only a little rice."

Beri-beri is caused by the absence of vitamin B, the antineuritic vitamin, in diet. It is prevalent in the Far East, in the Philippines and formerly in Newfoundland. In the East and the Philippines, the deficiency is due to the fact that the staple diet of the people is often highly-polished rice while, in Newfoundland, in winter time, the diet of the fishing folk was, in former times, frequently just bread and tea. Dr. Donald McI. Johnson, who was with the Grenfell Mission in Labrador, tells me that the Mission tried unsuccessfully for many years to persuade the fishermen of Newfoundland to substitute whole wheat flour for refined wheat flour in their bread with a view to the elimination of beri-beri.

Whenever undermilled rice and whole wheat flour have been substituted for highly-polished rice and refined wheat flour in the diets of people afflicted with beri-beri, a remarkable change for the better has taken place in their condition.

The Japs stubbornly refused to make the necessary changes in our diet to fight beri-beri. The principal constituent of our diet was polished rice and this was only supplemented by a few vegetables and a little tough meat.

I produce the evidence for the causes of beri-beri because, when I arrived back in London after my imprisonment, several highly-placed officers tried to convince me that our illness in Rangoon was due to malnutrition generally and not to vitamin B deficiency. I disagreed with them strenuously then, and all my subsequent reading and research on the subject has convinced me that not only are my conclusions right, but also that they are borne out by the findings of everyone who has made a specialised study of this disease.

A great deal of my time was spent in devising means of

fighting beri-beri. If it had not been, I doubt very much if we should have got the disease under even the limited control that we were able to establish. We adopted several methods and made various experiments.

The first method was to try to bring about an improvement in the diet. This we were able to accomplish by purchasing food from outside the jail, through the agency of men on the working parties. These men received a regular small wage and this, supplemented by what the officers could get released from their pay, was used to purchase extra rations, which we ensured were not deficient in vitamin B.

We were also able, during the first year of our imprisonment, to raise some wild spinach, radishes, maize and cabbages in the garden of No. 3 Block. Later the Japs took the control of this garden out of our hands and this source of supply virtually ceased, for the ground became quite exhausted, as it was never properly dug or manured.

Power, too, grew a few papaya trees from seed, but the fruit never properly fertilised and had little flavour. The fruit we were able to use, however, by getting the cooks to make jam and chutney out of it, a procedure we also adopted with soursops and green mangoes that the men were able to purchase outside.

We did not establish any effective contact with the Dutch prisoners from the East Indies, who were in the jail with us. They had their own medical staff and all that we knew was that they suffered very much worse than we did through beri-beri. It may well be that their doctors had not been through the same intensive courses in tropical medicine that R.A.M.C. officers posted to the East were given. It is doubtful if the average British medical practitioner would be able to deal with a case of beri-beri, without reference to his books, and no reference books were available in Rangoon Jail!

Perhaps the most successful experiment in preventive medicine that was carried through in Rangoon Jail was the bean-germinating station we established in the Central Water Tower. This provided us with a fair supply of beans, rich in vitamin B, although we never had enough to stamp out the disease, only to keep it under some sort of control.

The centre was under the charge of Corporal Tweedie of the Cameronians, one of the most useful men in the whole jail. He was able to get very little sleep, for his bean-germinating work involved his being called every three hours during the night by the Japanese guards to visit the centre, and he was unfortunate enough to have a name that the Japanese could pronounce. They had considerable difficulty with many British names but Tweedie they could manage; so often, when they wanted a man for any task, they took the line of least resistance and called for poor Tweedie.

The beans had to be weighed out, in the presence of Japanese guards, before they were issued and Tweedie was in constant trouble for making over-issues to the British and American blocks. He took his punishment well and was always appropriating little delicacies, such as vegetables and sugar, which he distributed amongst the sick officers and men.

The Japs never knew quite what to make of Tweedie, for he was a law unto himself. He came into closer contact with the guards than most people through his position at the bean-germinating centre and he thought nothing of visiting the other Blocks, when he was so minded, at considerable personal risk, to see his sick comrades and to hand them little things that he had acquired. He would bring back with him scraps of information he had picked up from prisoners in other compounds and from new arrivals in 'solitary'. He maintained quite close liaison with the Chinese and the Indians and even obtained information

Allied Prisoners of War have their last meal of rice before being taken away to Base Camp

Prisoners who marched out of Rangoon Jail at Pegu

sometimes from the Jap guards themselves. Tweedie was a great morale raiser and, in spite of some beatings, got away with things that the rest of us would not have dared to attempt.

I decided to demonstrate to my fellow prisoners Vitamin B deficiency and to show that it was caused by a rice diet. I did this from a conviction that men would be able to fight beri-beri better, if they had shown to them clearly the causes of the disease and the methods of prevention. We carried out these demonstrations under the very noses of the Jap guards and they never suspected what we were doing.

First of all we determined to capture some pigeons. There were a number of them nesting in the roof of No. 5 Block (the 'solitary' block) and it was their habit to come down into the garden of No. 3 Block to feed and drink. When I talked to the medical orderlies about the possibility of trapping some for experiments, I was delighted to find that one of them, L/Cpl. Hancock, was something of a pigeon-fancier in civilian life. He took charge of the operation of catching the pigeons, and the other orderlies erected a pigeon house from bits of wood, netting wire, sackings and other odds-and-ends. We had some twenty birds.

We decided to put some of the pigeons on a rice diet. Then we watched to see whether they developed symptoms of beri-beri. During the next few days, there was considerable excitement—it provided a new interest for the men. Within four to seven days, all the pigeons showed signs of beri-beri. Their movements became less and less active and some remained crouched on their perches until they fell off. The sheen disappeared from their feathers and the characteristic quick blink of the eyelid of the pigeon became lethargic. Some were sick and vomited; others developed a head retraction; a few could not walk across the floor of the cage but lay there with their claws closed;

they were unable to spread them but swayed from side to side on their 'knees', in order to move about from the water dish to the rice dish. One or two seemed unwilling or unable to move at all, even when they were disturbed.

When the symptoms had developed fully, I changed the diet. I fed some of the pigeons on rice bran, some on wheat and some on germinated bean shoots.

The pigeons who got wheat recovered much quicker than the rest and those who got rice bran recovered very slowly indeed. One hen pigeon on wheat, after only four days of treatment, recovered sufficiently to attract the attention of a male, also on wheat. We allowed them out of their separate compartments, once we started them on wheat diets, and the result was that two eggs were laid and hatched out in due course. Neither of the offspring showed any sign of beri-beri.

We could have done more experiments with these pigeons but the Japs suddenly suspected that we were using them to send messages—to whom I would not know! They ordered that the birds should be destroyed immediately and we had to comply with the order.

Having discovered that wheat was the most effective diet for beri-beri, the problem was to obtain wheat to apply our findings. The wheat for the pigeons had been a comparatively simple matter, for it had been brought in the required small quantities by working parties from the Veterinary Stables outside the jail. Bringing it in, to feed men, was a very much more difficult problem.

Nevertheless, we ventured in faith and were able to get wheat for two months. Private Bryson, an Australian, and Sergeant Martin, in the hospital kitchen, were closely associated with me in this endeavour but the main credit must go to those loyal fellows who, day after day, went out on working parties and came back with their pockets crammed with wheat from the stables. They completely deceived the Japs who never realised that pounds of their wheat were being stolen in this way every day.

We were now able to put the really bad beri-beri cases on a special diet. Martin made wheat porridge for them at breakfast by boiling the wheat with skim milk powder. A ration of gruel was eaten separately with some *juggaree* syrup. At midday, 'bradies' were made from chopped, boiled vegetable and bean shoots, pickled in salt solution. For the evening meal, the patients had either a fish-pie or a cottage-pie, made from ground wheat husks, a little meat and vegetables. They also got at various times a few wheat-cakes, spinach water, well-salted, and the inevitable 'char'.

Shortly before our patients were all transferred to No. 6 Block hospital, the wheat supply ran out and we were back where we started from. This was one of the most heart-rending experiences I had in jail. If only the Japs would have allowed us even a little wheat, we could have saved so many lives, but they took no notice of my urgent and constant representations in this matter.

One effective form of treatment we were able to give to beri-beri cases was muscle-control exercises. These were introduced by a prisoner, Private 'Skeeter' Jones, who had been a member of Tommy Farr's training school and who carried about with him a tattered text-book on the subject. 'Skeeter' worked very hard indeed with his classes for officers and men, suffering from beri-beri diarrhoea, in an attempt to tone up their abdominal muscles and to raise the intestinal tone of the alimentary canal. There is no doubt at all that these exercises restored a degree of tone to the abdominal and intestinal musculature. Jones would have done even better, had the men not been in such a low nervous and physical condition. His treatment required the closest attention and concentration by his pupils, before complete success could be achieved. It also required assiduous practice.

Incidentally, I still carry through the exercises taught me by 'Skeeter' Jones. What was an advantage in Rangoon Jail is an advantage today: the exercises require no apparatus. The training consists of learning the muscles of the body and their uses and then of causing them to contract by an effort of the will, without strain. First, this is done on both sides of the body, then on the left side alone, followed by a contraction of the muscles on the right side of the body alone. It can be done as many times as desired and whenever one has a minute or two to spare. I attribute my absence of middle-aged spread in the sixties to the muscle control exercises, shown to me by 'Skeeter' Jones in Rangoon Jail.

I shall always remember the pitiful sights I witnessed in the hospital, day after day, as prisoner after prisoner slipped out of life through beri-beri. It was devastating for a doctor to know that he could have saved life so easily and to be denied the means of doing so.

One morning, a young soldier, a fine boy, said to me, as I was going round the hospital: "Oh, sir, I can see two of you."

I forced a smile and replied: "That's a pity, surely one of me is bad enough." I made the joke with difficulty, for I knew that the lad was suffering from double vision—the beginning of his final coma. Yet he smiled to me, after my remark, and then settled down into his long last sleep.

I often used to watch a man named Bartram moving by with his working party. He was of exceptional physique, over six feet tall and with a magnificent body. I saw him become a walking skeleton before my eyes within a few weeks. He was dying from inability to absorb the kind of nourishment he was getting.

The day he was admitted to hospital, this splendid fellow turned to me and said in a gentle voice: "I am so sorry, sir, I am letting you down."

To.- Col. K.P. Mackenzie. R.A.M.C

A small appreciation sir
This morn we bring to you
To help you on your daily task
Of pulling people through

And when the battle's o'er sir
The smell of powder gone
We're going to be among the first
To thank you with **WELL DONE!**

from the men of the 2ND BATTALION

Kings Own Yorkshire Light Infantry

Rangoon   1-1 44

New Year Card received by the Author, 1st January, 1944.

113

I knew that Bartram was dying but I answered: "Now don't talk nonsense, man. If you could only manage to eat a little each day, we could get you pulled up in no time. Is there anything you particularly fancy? I will try and get it for you."

"I'd love a bit of pork, sir," he said. I managed to get one of the men to buy a small piece from outside. When I saw him on my rounds later, I asked Bartram how he was and he remarked: "Oh, sir, that pork was grand."

I told him that I would try and get him some more pork the next day but it was then too late, for Bartram had finished his journey.

I suppose that it is true to say that the great majority of us in Rangoon Jail suffered from neurasthenia in greater or less degree. Manifestations of this were the way in which prison rumours carried like wildfire, and the manner in which otherwise sensible and friendly men would indulge in carping and destructive criticism.

I sometimes used to make remarks to my fellow prisoners, just to see how they would be distorted, before they arrived back to me within a day or two. I would then take pleasure in pricking that particular bubble, for I considered that it was a sensible thing to do to demonstrate how a simple statement could become magnified and distorted.

It was difficult to know what to believe, for we lived in a world sealed off from normal channels of communication. In such a place men came to repeat things, not from malice, but from a desire to revert to the machinery of the normal means of communication of information.

I believed that Lieutenant Lowry-Corry of the Royal Inniskilling Fusiliers had been taken out in front of his company and bayoneted by the Japs after capture, for a Fusilier in the jail told me that this had happened. I was, therefore, somewhat surprised, after I had returned to London, to go into Lock's the hatters, in St. James' Street, on 6th July, 1945, and to find Lieutenant Lowry-Corry in there buying a hat!

Some of the officers became regular 'Nosey Parkers'. They would go to the hospital and talk to the men, telling them what was wrong with them and giving all manner of extraordinary advice about treatment.

A typical example occurred one morning on sick parade. One of the men said to me: "Sir, I have renal colic." I knew he had nothing of the sort, so I replied: "Well, now you have diagnosed your complaint, you had better cure it. I am unlikely to be able to do so, for I have only some quinine tablets, some copper sulphate and no instruments." He went away quite hurt.

On another occasion, I felt constrained to make a public protest. We had had many cases of jungle-sores and ring-worm and the 'experts' were airing their views freely on how to treat these diseases. The simple fact was that we had not had sufficient soap and water to wash properly for weeks. I took the opportunity to address the compound on the subject and opened up by saying: "I am so sorry to have to speak, but I think I ought to make it clear that, out of our compound strength of two hundred and eighty-three at the present time, we are fortunate in having two hundred and eighty-two doctors amongst us. I am in a minority of one—the only layman!" Afterwards, I feared that the prison mentality must be getting hold of me too.

Several accidents overtook our prisoners in the city of Rangoon. Corporal Caton was badly injured when the motor lorry, in which his party were returning from work, capsized, when taking a corner. He sustained a crush fracture of the pelvis and internal injuries. We had no hope of getting an X-ray and, therefore, had to concentrate upon conservative treatment, but we were able to nurse him back to health.

Another soldier, working in an underground shelter,

that was being excavated for the Nip prison staff underneath one of the blocks, was electrocuted when he came into contact with one of the live electric cables. The party had been warned by Sergeant-Major McCabe to keep away from the wires. I found two of the party applying artificial respiration but, on examination, I found that the man was dead.

Two officers suggested afterwards that artificial respiration might have been continued for longer, as they had heard of cases where men had been brought back to life after twenty-four or forty-eight hours. I told them shortly that I had pronounced life extinct and that I should be glad if they could quote a case of a man who had been brought back to life in these circumstances! I assured them that they were welcome to carry on artificial respiration for as many days as they liked, if they thought it would do any good. They apologised to me in a day or two, but the incident showed that the nerves of all of us were getting a little frayed.

One of the most frustrating orders given by the Japs was when they decided that the Indian Block M.O., Captain Sudan, and I should bring all our sick over to the M.I. hut, outside the central Water Tower daily. I was told to bring a 'stethoscope' with me so that they could see me examining the patients. I managed to evade this particular order by bringing the 'stethoscope' for a morning or two and then adopting the procedure of telling the Japs that we had no sick for examination, only cases for dressing. I never did find out the meaning of this order, but it caused us the maximum inconvenience, without, as far as I could see, benefiting the Japs in any way. We were greatly inconvenienced by Nips passing in and out of the small hut and constantly peering at us. They were actuated by curiosity rather than by pursuit of knowledge.

This ridiculous sick parade procedure continued until

the liberation. I worked in the hut and Sudan did his dressings outside the window on a chair and on an empty packing case. We had to pass all the equipment we had in and out of the window to each other. The small hut was always crammed and, every few minutes, we had to stand to attention, when a Jap came in or passed. These were particularly irritating interruptions, for the Nips were always driving us to finish our dressings, before the working parties paraded. Some men just had to go out to Rangoon to perform coolie labour without receiving attention and this meant having an extra dressing parade in the evenings.

Operations and Emergencies

IT is part of the life of an Army medical officer to deal with anything that comes along and, abroad and in time of war, this has sometimes to be done in difficult and unusual circumstances.

Even so, I should never have imagined that my war service would have involved applying my surgical skill under the kind of conditions that were on several occasions necessitated by the circumstances in which we found ourselves in Rangoon Jail.

A specially tragic episode concerns the crew of an American bomber.

Early one afternoon, we had seen from the windows of Hobson's room, an old, captured, five-ton lorry arrive outside the Solitary Block. Out of this, a number of heavily-bandaged human beings were decanted and then helped and carried into the block. That evening, the 'bush telegraph' buzzed with the information that we had, amongst us, the crew of an American aircraft, that had been engaged upon a bombing mission and had been hit and forced to make a 'crash-landing' outside Rangoon.

At a later date, I discovered that Major Werhner, who was the captain of the bomber, had, on landing, rushed to the exit door and dragged his crew of six from the blazing wreck. They were all, of course, very severely burnt about the face, head, neck, hands, arms and legs; and their clothing was practically burnt off them. The only one who escaped comparatively unhurt from this holocaust was Major Werhner, himself, who was in good shape except for a slight degree of concussion. Werhner, after his allotted span in 'solitary', was put into No. 3 Block, in Hobson's room, and he thus became one of us for the remainder of our stay in jail.

His companions were less fortunate than he. It was natural that the type of treatment they received in 'solitary' did nothing to ameliorate the serious condition they were in on arrival. Throughout the night, we could hear these poor fellows, moaning in their agony and we knew that, as they lay there, they had not even the sparse comforts of proper beds and blankets.

It was, however, the fifth day of their presence in camp before I was told by the Jap medical orderly, whom we called 'the Paper Boy', to follow him. He led me the short distance across to the Solitary Block.

When I arrived there, I saw a sight that I shall never forget as long as I live. This block, like the others, had along one side of it a verandah—the usual flimsy structure with concrete floor and sloping wooden slats to form a roof. Five of the unfortunate Americans had been dragged out of the cells and laid on the verandah, for me to see them there. Two of them were lying quietly on the floor, with only strips of rush matting between them and the concrete. The other three, however, had their heads completely swathed in bandages so that there were only openings left for the mouth and nose. They could not see and were crawling about on the dusty floor blindly, like badly-bitten animals. The burns on their necks, heads and faces had been dressed with vaseline, on top of which sheets of grease-proof paper and layers of gauze had been placed. The grease-proof paper had been most ineffective and the vaseline had soaked right through the bandages, with the result that a horrible clotted mass of sand and dirt from the ground and grease from the dressings covered the entire necks and heads of the airmen. They had been crawling around their cells for four days in this condition, supporting themselves on their knees and elbows. They were unable to see, unable to use their hands and unable to feed themselves and were still dressed in the same burnt clothing that they had been wearing when captured. One of them later told me that he had tried to lick rice from a dish and off the filthy floor of the cell, just as a cat or dog would, in a desperate effort to keep alive, but that he had acquired no great skill in feeding himself this way.

In the meantime, however, I was in the Solitary Block and the rules of the prison camp prevailed. I was allowed to examine the patients, but not to speak to them.

The first airman I looked at was in a profound state of collapse from the spread of general infection throughout his body. Clearly, he had not long to live. I realised that the greatest kindness I could render him was not to disturb him further.

I turned my attention to the others. Before long, I was convinced that this was not a one-man job and I took my stand. I insisted that 'the Paper Boy' should get Major Ramsay along to help me. This was done, fortunately without undue delay, and, after we had each examined these unfortunate fellows in turn, we held a consultation.

We formed the same opinion about what should be done and it was the opinion that any doctor in his senses would have formed. We realised that all these men were in a deplorable and dangerous state and I sent a message, through the interpreter, O'Hari San, to the Camp Commandant. I announced that, if any of the men were to have a chance of life, it was essential that they should be transferred to a Japanese hospital in Rangoon without delay and that they should be given proper nursing attention there.

This was an entire waste of energy. O'Hari San came back within three-quarters of an hour with a point blank refusal.

While the interpreter was away, Ramsay and I, with the concurrence of 'the Paper Boy' proceeded to dress the wounds of the patients. We left alone, however, the man whom I have already mentioned, who was too far gone to benefit from any ministrations.

It took us quite an hour, in each case, to remove the old bandages, clean up the sorry mess that lay beneath them and put on a fresh dressing of gauze soaked in acriflavine, and to bandage up again with such odd pieces of cloth as were available to us. What a shock it was to me to find that all the burnt areas, as well as the cuts and abrasions, on the scalps, ears, eyes and noses of our patients, were crawling with maggots. There were maggots in the nostrils, maggots in the cheek wounds and maggots between the fingers as well. Ramsay and I picked out these horrible larvae one by one, with the aid of an old pair of Japanese dissecting forceps.

When we had cleaned them up a bit, I put forward the suggestion that, if the Commandant would permit it, I would take three of the men into No. 3 Block hospital while Ramsay would take the other two into No. 6 Block hospital.

O'Hari San went away again. He returned half an hour later. This time the answer was more favourable. We could take them into our hospitals on the usual conditions for prisoners in 'solitary'. The other prisoners were not to speak to them, so that there could be no risk of information passing one way or the other.

We readily agreed to this. It was a relief to me to get the three patients under my care and I was able to arrange, by taking these from other men, that they got fresh clothing, blankets and mosquito nets for the night. I also saw that they were fed in a proper manner with such meagre rations as we could provide. I was particularly fortunate in that I had, in reserve, two ampoules of morphine solution for injections. These had been salvaged several months before from some fresh arrivals, all of whom made it a custom loyally to hand over to me any medical supplies that they happened to bring in with them.

This precious pain-killing drug has seldom, if ever, been put to better use. I injected the two worst cases, bringing them the peace of mind and release from suffering that they deserved and craved. It was, however, too late for me to do anything more than this. One of my charges died during the night.

The second lingered on for forty-eight hours. He was a brave man, sane and courageous to the end, despite his desperate plight. How he maintained his reason, I just do not know, for both his eyes had been destroyed, eaten away by maggots, which, when we had first seen him, filled the whole of his orbital cavities.

The third patient, Sergeant Daley, an unusually burly type of American, provided a more cheerful story. Amazingly enough, he recovered completely, after a gruelling ordeal of many weeks. Sometimes, his wounds had to be dressed as often as three times a day and, each time, a fresh crop of maggots had to be picked out of them. As he started to recover, his hands and forearms had to be put into extemporised wooden splints, in order to prevent contraction and webbing of the fingers. But he was a stout-hearted patient and was always pathetically grateful for anything we could do for him. He was actually going out with the ordinary working parties doing coolie labour in Rangoon, before we were released. Such is the resilience of the human frame and the human spirit!

The two airmen, under Ramsay's care in No. 6 Block hospital, died. The miracle was that we were able to save the life of one.

Another American airman was the recipient of my surgical attention in a different fashion, some two or three months later. I was sent for one day by the Jap medical lieutenant from Rangoon, who visited the jail occasionally.

I was conducted into his august presence by the small, bespectacled, chattering, puffy-faced O'Hari San.

The lieutenant was seated at a table in a bare room in the Central Water Tower. I marched in and made my obeisances to him and he started to talk to O'Hari San in an unpleasant whining voice. I disliked this medical officer intensely but I could see that he wanted me to help him, and that accordingly he did not intend to be too objectionable on this occasion.

A conversation started. O'Hari San translated:

"The lieutenant asks you that you will help him to operate."

"Tell the lieutenant that I am willing to do so," I replied.

I noticed, on my entry, that the doctor was studying a Japanese text-book on surgery, in somewhat perplexed fashion. Now his relief on hearing my reply was obvious. Perhaps, I thought, the lieutenant is not a very experienced surgeon!

"Would the lieutenant like *me* to operate?" I asked the interpreter.

When this was translated, the relief of the Jap was painfully obvious. But the reply when it came was condescending:

"The lieutenant will permit that."

"May I be allowed to have Major Ramsay to help me?"

"The lieutenant will permit that, also."

"May I see my case, before the operation?"

This request received a different reception.

"No, you may not," came the sharp answer, "the lieutenant will not allow you to see him."

I was then curtly dismissed with the unhappy thought that I had committed myself to operate on some unfortunate being, whom I had never seen and of whom I knew nothing.

My anxiety on this score was, however, somewhat allayed when I was sent for about an hour later, to visit the Water Tower again. There I found that one of the entrance alcoves to the Tower had been converted into a very primitive and highly extemporised operating theatre. There was just room in its precincts for the iron hospital bed which was to act as an operating table and for another table on which to place the necessary instruments and dressings. It was to be *alfresco* surgery, for the alcove, of course, lay open, not only to the stifling air of the early afternoon, but also to all the dust of the compound with its accompanying germs and risks of infection.

I concealed my anxiety and dismay about these conditions, however, as I saw being conducted towards me a dark-haired man of medium height, whom I could easily discern, from his tattered uniform, as being an American airman. He came from No. 8 Block, where they were imprisoned, entirely separated from the British. I was given the strictest instructions that I must only talk to him within such limits as could easily be understood by the interpreter and that I must confine my conversation absolutely to such necessary interchange of words, as were permitted by the interpreter for me to diagnose his condition. It was only, therefore, at a much later date that I found out that the name of my patient was Air Force Sergeant Richard Montgomery.

Montgomery had been hit in the wrist by a splinter of ack-ack shell, when his plane had been brought down a week or two previously. The Japs in the front line had amputated his forearm, just above the wrist. The result had not been happy. When I saw him the amputated stump was filthy and septic, infected ends of bones were protruding from it and Montgomery was suffering from severe nerve pains, going right up his arm.

I had two clear choices. One was to amputate higher up the forearm; the other was to disarticulate at the elbow-joint and remove the whole forearm. The second choice involved, of course, a more drastic and crippling operation. My decision rested upon two points.

The first came out in my preliminary talk with the Japanese lieutenant, when I explained the alternatives to him.

"The lieutenant says," interpreted O'Hari San, "that, if you amputate again in the forearm, and that wound goes septic, then there are no more dressings left for you, when you have to remove at the elbow."

That sounded decisive but, had I still had any doubts, they would have been settled when I saw the instruments at my disposal. These were a small collection, taken from a captured British Army Field Surgical Pannier, consisting of four bluntish-looking scalpels, four small artery forceps, two tiny needle-holders, two 'rat-toothed' dissecting forceps, a few rusty-looking, half-curved, non-cutting surgical needles, some strands of fine horsehair, a quantity of surgical silk in ampoules with a hank of fishing gut in a tube, two hypodermic syringes and a medium-sized bottle of methylated spirits. In addition to these, there was a saw—just an ordinary butchers' saw, such as is used for cutting meat. If I had amputated through the forearm, I would, of course, have had to saw through the two bones of this part. If, on the other hand, I disarticulated at the elbow, I would not need to use a saw. I resolved to dis-articulate at the elbow. I am very glad I did not have to employ that saw.

I was allowed to say sufficient to the patient to inform him that I was carrying out the operation with the greatest possible reluctance and with misgiving, because of the miserable facilities at my disposal. I spared him the details of the reasons for my decision. I merely told him what was quite true—that I was operating in an attempt to save his life and that I would be as gentle as possible.

The patient lay down on the iron bedstead, still wearing his dusty boots. The Japs found me, thank heaven, two ampoules of two per cent Novocaine, under normal conditions used as a dental anaesthetic, but now a Godsend to me as I could use it for local anaesthesia, in the absence of a general anaesthetic. I considered myself fortunate at that moment that, in my younger days, when I was House Surgeon to the great Sir Henry Gray, at the Aberdeen Royal Infirmary, I had had a chief who specialised in this particular form of anaesthesia and I had acquired considerable experience in it, myself, under his tuition.

Working under these conditions, we started. I cut slowly away and infiltrated with fresh injections of the anaesthetic as I cut, while the Jap medical orderly, Yamamoto, applied the tourniquet—applied it very efficiently, I have to admit—and Major Ramsay helped me. The lieutenant stood by in helpless and bewildered fashion. The operation took an hour and a half, by the end of which time I had removed the forearm and provided a good flap of skin to fold over the lower end of the humerus bone. The stump was bandaged, the tourniquet removed and my patient was conducted back to his block. There were, of course, no such refinements as operating trolleys. The poor chap had to stagger back, assisted by two comrades. I returned, unthanked by the Japs, to No. 3 Block.

This was the first and last time I saw Sergeant Richard Montgomery.

Next day, I asked the Jap medical sergeant if my patient could be brought over to the block for me to see him. I was not only anxious as to his progress, but also I wanted to inject some more Novocaine into his stump, if the nerve-endings were still proving painful. The sergeant promised that this would be done, but nothing happened.

I was left without news, not even knowing who my patient was—the story was going round the compound that he was at least a General!—or what progress he was making. Three weeks later, I had the opportunity of asking this same sergeant again if I could see the patient and how the arm was. By this time, still having no news, I was watching out for the all too familiar signs of a funeral procession from the direction of the American block. The sergeant answered simply: "Arm no good, MacKenzie no good." This did not make me feel any more cheerful!

I heard nothing directly but, through diverse channels in the next few months, the news came that Montgomery's arm had recovered completely and it was a source of comfort and joy to me to receive grateful messages and thanks from him in the same way.

I have recorded that I did not see Montgomery again and it was, therefore, a special delight to me, several years later, when I was a free man again, to pick up the *Daily Telegraph* and read the following extract in Peterborough's column:

"*Prosthetic Limbs.*

An indication of the remarkable efficiency of artificial limbs in America is the fact that disabled ex-Servicemen, equipped with these limbs, are being drafted back into the Forces.

There is the case, for instance, of Master-Sergeant Richard Montgomery. He lost his left arm and has just rejoined the Army Air Force as a radio operator. His 'prosthetic' arm performs nearly all the functions of a natural one.

Montgomery baled out of his plane over Burma, and in doing so lost his left hand. Owing to neglect in a Japanese prison camp in Rangoon, gangrene set in.

His only hope was to have the whole arm amputated. There were no medical facilities in the prison camp. A British officer, Colonel K. P. MacKenzie, offered to perform the operation. He did so, without anaesthetics, and saved Sergeant Montgomery's life.

The sergeant has never seen Colonel Mackenzie since Rangoon was retaken from the Japanese in May, 1945. He speaks of him with the highest admiration and affection, however, and would like to get in touch with him.

Perhaps Colonel Mackenzie is a Peterborough reader, or is known to one."

A less happy outcome attended the other major operation, which I conducted within the confines of the jail—that on the Chinese officer—Major-General Chi.

Some months after we arrived, Block No. 1 had been occupied by Chinese prisoners, who towards the end of 1942 had been captured, while attempting to infiltrate down from the North.

We, of course, were not allowed to communicate with them but Hobson had got to know something of General Chi, through being present with him at conferences with the Commandant. He was a fine type of Chinese officer. He had charming manners and had served his country long and faithfully in her many vicissitudes. Both his manners and his excellent command of the English language can be seen in the following letter which he sent to Brigadier Hobson in appreciation of the service that our Indian Army medical officers had rendered the troops under his command in the jail. He also knew Japanese well, a fact that he most successfully concealed from our captors.

"To Brigadier General Hobson
    through Captain B. N. Sudan, B.A.M.C.

March 4, '44.
Dear Sir,
    I beg to inform you that for more than six months our sick men, with the permission of the Japanese, have been placed under the medical care of four British Medical Officers, Capts. Sudan, Pillay, Thomas and Rao, all Indian officers of the British Army. Among them Capt. B. N. Sudan's services have been especially valuable to us. During this period we have not had a single death and three of our soldiers were virtually snatched away from the very jaws of death—all through the effort of that good officer. In consideration of the difficulties imposed upon by the Japanese and the regrettable lack of medical facilities at present, he has certainly done a great deal. It would indeed be ungrateful on my part not to acknowledge the very considerable services he has rendered to us. It is therefore, only just for me to bring his excellent services to the notice of the most senior British officer here and to express our appreciation and thanks thereby.

I will be ready and only too glad to bear testimony to the above statement when called upon to do so at any time after the war if I am lucky enough to survive it.

> I beg to remain,
> Respectfully yours,
> H. C. CHI
> Maj. Gen. Chinese."

It was not long after writing this letter that the General was stabbed, while lying in his bunk at eleven o'clock one night, by one of his own soldiers, whose allegiance had been suborned by representatives of the puppet Nanking Government. These people visited the Chinese Block from time to time with a view to persuading the Chinese prisoners to join their own traitorous faction. In this instance, they were all too successful. Chi received a deep penetrating wound in the middle of the abdomen, just above the navel, from a sharp, single-bladed knife. With prompt surgical action, such a wound should present no undue danger but, unfortunately, no such action was taken, owing to the callous delays of our jailers.

We were awakened at the time by the voices of the Japs, as they went to and from the Central Water Tower, fetching medical supplies. It was not, however, until the next morning that we learnt that General Chi had been stabbed.

On the afternoon of the second day, O'Hari San summoned me to the Water Tower again where I found the same lieutenant sitting in the same bare room.

The interpreter addressed me:

"The lieutenant says that General Chi is wounded in the liver and he wants you to operate upon him."

The whine in the lieutenant's voice, as he spoke to O'Hari San, seemed to me to have an even more harassed tone in it than I had been aware of in our previous interview over Sergeant Montgomery.

This point-blank request took me aback somewhat, however. I told him, as politely as I knew how, through the interpreter, that it was not usual to contemplate an operation of such gravity as this, without first having had the opportunity of examining the patient. Surely, I suggested, General Chi should be taken to a proper operating theatre in a military hospital.

This suggestion, however, did not please the lieutenant.

"I want you to operate on him," he shouted, scowling at the interpreter, as he spoke.

Again I tried to insist that I should be allowed to see the patient and to form my own opinion, whether an operation was absolutely necessary, in the conditions under which I knew it would have to be performed. I knew through 'the grapevine' that General Chi had, in fact, asked to be seen by a British medical officer.

My attitude infuriated the Japanese lieutenant. He began cursing me in Japanese. As he did so, he rose to his feet and reached over to the table where O'Hari San was sitting. He picked up a round wooden ruler, some two feet long. This he started to brandish over my head, still showering curses upon me. I expected to have my head battered in at any moment but he thought better of it and just resumed his seat, banging the ruler on the table and continuing to curse in his unpleasant, whining voice.

"Bow to the lieutenant," hissed the interpreter through his rabbit teeth.

This I did in the customary ceremonial fashion. Then, assuming this to be, as it usually was, the implied command to leave, I started to walk out of the room.

"Come back," snapped O'Hari San. "Bow to the lieutenant again."

I turned round and wearily walked back to the table, and once more performed the same ceremony, only to be greeted by a flood of Japanese abuse.

"*Ukinasi*, get away," hissed the interpreter again.

I turned about again and left. Thus ended this highly unusual professional consultation.

Meanwhile, of course, General Chi's condition was not improving.

I heard nothing more until the next morning when a Jap medical orderly came up to me, with a dressing pad from General Chi's wound. This had been sent by Captain Rao of the Indian Medical Service, who had that day been detailed to look after the General. I did not now need to see the patient. The discharge which soaked the dressing consisted of highly offensive faeculent fluid from the peritoneal cavity and partly digested bowel contents, amongst which were a number of chilli seeds. It was perfectly obvious to me what had happened. The wound had pierced the bowel of General Chi. An operation was an immediate necessity. I sent back a message to Rao to this effect, suggesting that the Commandant and the Jap medical officer be informed immediately.

I later ascertained that this was done. Despite the urgency of the matter, however, it was four o'clock in the afternoon before the Japanese medical lieutenant appeared at the gate of our compound and demanded to see me. I told him what I had already informed Captain Rao—namely that there was undoubted evidence of a bowel lesion, with a virulent infection of the peritoneum, that must have been going on now for forty-eight hours. I added that this was a very long time for such an infection to proceed untreated and that Chi's chances had become very poor.

The lieutenant went away to consult the Commandant and returned, ten minutes later, with the renewed request that I should operate. I agreed to this, stipulating that Major Ramsey should again assist me.

The operation took place within the next hour. I have already described the site and the conditions of operating and the instruments and other facilities that were available. They were the same as in the case of the previous operation upon Sergeant Montgomery. I managed, however, to add a hank of cotton thread, which I had taken from our tailor in No. 3 Block, to my store of ligatures. Fortunately, on this occasion the Japs did produce two pairs of rubber gloves. This was a great relief as such abdominal cases can be very infectious and dangerous to handle.

We did have operating gowns, but there was a total absence of the usual paraphernalia of sterile towels and dressings, which, under civilised conditions, we consider essential for any major operation.

We started to boil the instruments and to scrub up, as well as we could. While we were doing so, the patient was carried in.

General Chi did not look well. Unaccustomed as I was to patients of his race and colour, I could see at a glance that his face was pinched and fevered. His grave and courteous manner, however, still lay upon him, just as if he was at the peak of his fortunes, instead of in the piteous state in which we now met him.

It did not take long to examine him or to sum up the benefits of the efforts at treatment by the Japanese lieutenant, who had previously made an attempt to relieve Chi's condition. This 'brilliant' surgeon had, in his efforts to drain the infected cavity, merely succeeded in sticking a small piece of drainage tube into the skin of the abdomen and had anchored it there with a couple of stitches. The tube, however, was merely skin-deep in the wound and was not inside the peritoneal cavity at all. In these circumstances, it was not the slightest use.

I had once again been warned that I must only talk to the General in terms that the interpreter could hear and understand. Indeed, such was the gathering in this confined place, that I would have been smart to do anything else. In addition to the patient, Major Ramsay, and myself, there were present, the Japanese medical lieutenant, and Yamamoto, who had helped me so well at my previous operation, two interpreters and the General's Chinese orderly. To this throng was added the august person of the Commandant, himself, and he was accompanied by a sergeant.

No surgeon, however famous, ever had a more appreciative gallery. It was soon clear that this was a Red Letter day in jail life, as I started my work, surrounded by grinning yellow faces. The Commandant stationed himself on my left and, so eagerly did he watch the spectacle, that I could feel his breath on my arm and incidentally going down over my patient's wound as well.

The operation took an hour in all, but the story of it can be told briefly. I explained to General Chi that I would do the best I could and that I would hurt him as little as possible. I also assured him that, with the aid of the Novocaine at my disposal, there was a reasonable prospect of a painless operation. Then I proceeded, utilising the same anaesthetic technique as I had used previously.

My forebodings were borne out. I found that the small bowel had been perforated by the knife, so causing leakage of contents into the abdominal cavity and, consequently, inflammation and peritonitis. By this time, of course, it had become adherent to the abdominal wall and an inflamed mass of fatty omentum—the protective fatty apron of the abdominal contents—was glued to it as well. This I loosened away, releasing a considerable amount of filthy-smelling fluid. Into the cavity, I inserted a long drainage tube and stitched this in place. The liver, incidentally, I found quite undamaged. This part of the operation completed, I made a second opening for drainage in the midline in the lower part of the abdomen and stitched in a second tube to serve for irrigation and drainage. I then asked that Captain Rao be brought and I showed him how

I wanted the irrigations of saline carried out, through the tubes I had inserted.

The operation was over. I told the General that I was sorry that I could not do more for him. He understood.

The patient was taken away, the 'theatre' was cleared and the party started to disperse. The Commandant went into the neighbouring M.I. Room, however, where he waited until I walked in to put on my khaki shirt, after I had removed my gloves and washed my hands. He appeared extremely pleased. So much so that he asked me to sit down and have a cigarette which I was glad to accept—shades of Coshima! Others came in, Major Ramsay, the Jap medical lieutenant (now all smiles) with the Jap orderly and O'Hari San. I had never known the jail atmosphere more propitious. Through the interpreter, the Jap Commandant started to convey his congratulations and thanks and began to make conversation about our different styles of head-dress and so forth. The lieutenant also joined in, doing his best to make himself pleasant. He, like the others, could not smile enough. It was clear that a good time had been had by all—with the possible exception of the patient. Poor General Chi died thirty-six hours later. At the stage at which I was allowed to perform the operation, there was nothing that I could have done that would have saved his life.

The Commandant concluded the proceedings by inviting me to take tea with him. I had had enough. I was exhausted and dripping with sweat. I made the excuse that I wanted to return to the compound and wash and dry my clothing.

McLeod also performed some remarkably difficult operations in Rangoon Jail. I was not present at any of these but saw some of the results he obtained, when amputating without anaesthetics.

One case in which he achieved a wonderful result was

when he removed the leg of a sturdy little Welshman, Corporal J. Usher from Wrexham, just below the thigh. Thanks to the skill of McLeod, Usher made an excellent recovery and was amongst the party that was liberated— when the British eventually re-entered Rangoon.

" They also Serve . . ."

IT may well be that those who, during the War, were within hearing distance of the B.B.C. news bulletins, who read newspapers published at home and who maintained close contact with their families and friends were able to sustain, without undue difficulty, a resolute faith in Allied victory—in spite of the reverses and disappointments inflicted upon our armies from time to time. They could see the whole picture. All the resources of modern propaganda were directed towards the elevation of their morale and towards the encouragement of their minds and spirits.

Our case was very different. We were completely cut off from all reliable sources of news and had to dwell in a state of nagging uncertainty about the fate that might have overtaken those whom we loved and about the future of the countries to which we belonged.

We British prisoners were allowed to understand that the cities of the British Isles were being subjected to prolonged, intensive and successful bombing, that our soldiers were suffering defeat after defeat in the field and that the victory of the Axis powers was inevitable. It is to the infinite credit of my comrades that I never heard one of them express the opinion that there was any possibility of ultimate defeat. We held on stubbornly and steadfastly in the belief that, by behaving with dignity and refusing to allow the Japs to 'get us down', we were making some contribution to the common cause. It was not easy to maintain faith but we conditioned our minds to do so.

'The seasons came, the seasons passed
They watched their fellows die;
But still their thought was forward cast,
Their courage still was high.
Though tortured days and fevered nights
Their limbs alone were weak,
And year by year, they kept their cheer
And spoke as free men speak.'

What news of the progress of the war elsewhere we did receive, came through a paper that the Japanese published at Rangoon in English called *Greater Asia*, and nicknamed by us: *Blood and Mucus*. This was a propaganda sheet and it was launched, with a great flourish of trumpets by the Japanese, soon after we reached Rangoon Jail. Then it consisted of some twelve pages of closely-set material and highly-coloured news, glorifying the triumphs of Nippon. The effect of this paper might have been greater, if some of the photographs had not been so obviously faked. They would not have deceived a child. As the war progressed, the size of this newspaper decreased and the Japs ceased to make it freely available to us. Eventually, it dwindled to a single sheet of brownish paper, printed on one side only, containing snippets of war news and having no photographs. It is a clear indication of our hunger for news that this sheet was eagerly sought after and our working parties would buy used copies outside the jail from Indians and Burmans, whom they were able to contact, and would pay as much as two or three rupees for a single copy.

To most of us, the absence of accurate news about the war was a very serious deprivation but, to all of us, the absence of news about our homes and families was mental agony. None of our men fared much better than I did and my experience was that I received my first mail from Britain, consisting of three letters, on the first day of the twelfth month of the third year of my imprisonment. My second and last mail, consisting of seven letters, came about ten days later.

Soon after the officers were released from 'solitary' in September, 1942, we were paraded and were told to write a letter to our next-of-kin. We were instructed to make much favourable comment upon the Japanese-sponsored Greater East Asia Co-Prosperity Sphere. We all did this for we were desperately anxious to get some communication back to tell our relatives that we were still alive and holding on. We were not allowed to write home again until about a week after the receipt of our first mail. Then we were permitted to send a post-card of twenty-five words (the address to count as one word), written in block capitals. When we were writing these postcards, I remarked to some of my fellow-prisoners that I believed we should arrive home, ourselves, before the postcards did. I was quite right. I have now been home for several years but my postcard has not turned up yet!

During the whole time that I was in captivity my wife received no communication from me. She heard nothing from me in my own handwriting from my capture on 22nd February, 1942 until I walked into her Kensington flat, after breakfast, on 7th June, 1945. I have before me, as I write, two telegrams that told to her the whole story. The first is dated 28th March, 1942 and reads: 'Regret to inform you of notification from India that Colonel K. P. Mackenzie, M.B., R.A.M.C. was reported missing on 22nd February, 1942 letter follows—Under Secretary of State of War.' The second dated 17th May, 1945, has the message: 'From the War Office London 16/1555/B OS/3861M Pleased to state that Colonel K. P. Mackenzie, M.B. recovered from Japanese hands present address BHM Delhi letter follows—Under Secretary of State for War.' Here I shall comment, without prejudice, on the experiences of my wife and children, while I was a prisoner. The telegram informing my wife that I was missing was placed in the letter box of her home with a bundle of other letters and, as soon as I was posted as 'missing', all pay and allowances to my family ceased. My wife was told that she was not eligible for a pension, as my death was not proved and she was not even permitted to draw upon my accumulated pay, because I had not signed the necessary form.

She was first told to take her case to the Colonial Office, as I had been posted missing in Burma but was there informed that the matter was one for the India Office, as I had been serving with an Indian Division.

It all seems to have been an unnecessary muddle, and a cruel muddle at that, for the result of red tape and procrastination was that my family had to give up their house and became homeless for the rest of the war. Is it absolutely necessary in these circumstances that wives should have to add economic insecurity to all the emotional turmoil of learning that their husbands are victims of war and may never return?

Not only were we denied the luxury of correspondence and the ordinary amenities of life, which the European resident in the tropics is ordinarily accustomed to have, but we were faced with the situation that the Japanese would not allow the representatives of the International Red Cross at Geneva, or representatives from neutral countries, to enter any of the prisoner-of-war camps in Burma. Neither would they allow any Red Cross parcels into the country. This piece of petty spite was greatly resented by us for it would have cost the Nips nothing to do so and we knew, from our own experience before our capture, that prisoners in the hands of other enemies were allowed to have these parcels.

The Japanese seemed to have some difficulty in deciding exactly in what category as a place of incarceration Rangoon should be placed. Normally they referred to it as a jail and then one knew exactly where one was. Before we left Moulmein, however, we were assured that we were going to Rangoon Field Prison Camp, where we would be able to get pay and to be better fed. Our last Commandant, on the other hand, was at some pains to explain to us that the word 'jail' was not to be used by us. We were to be known as No. 5 Prisoners of War Concentration Camp. 'A rose by any other name would smell as sweet'!

Our jailers were quite as confused about the numbering of British prisoners. I have already told that, when we arrived at Rangoon, I was given the prison number 128. We were then told that we must wear a disc with this number on it on our shirts and, if we had no shirts, we were to wear it on our shorts or on the *fundoshis* (a type of Japanese 'G' string), with which we were issued.

Later, the Japs, to cover up the ravages caused by death, re-allotted to us new prison numbers. I now became No. 7 and Major Loring took over from C.S.M. McCabe the distinction of being Prisoner No. 1.

Subsequently, we were issued with tin number plates about 1½ inches by 2 inches, perforated by a wire with which to fix them on. The rank and nationality of the prisoner, in Japanese characters, was on the top and the Army service number of the prisoner was painted in black along the lower half. My plate bears my British Army personal number: 14221. These we were told to keep. What for, I do not know, for they were never put to any effective use.

A fourth alteration in the numbers was carried through, after we had all been made to sign an undertaking that we would not try to escape—the Japs were constantly calling upon us to sign undertakings of this sort. My number then became 676. The Japanese alone can explain the reason for this extraordinary procedure.

The pay that we received at Rangoon was a typical Japanese 'swindle'. The men got 10 cents a day for doing coolie labour, that is they received a basic wage of about twopence a day. The N.C.Os. received a little more than this. They were, however, able to get a relatively substantial increase in remuneration through the system that the Japs operated of giving a bonus to all men who worked for eight days on end, or more. Squadron Leader Duckenfield made himself responsible for maintaining the pay-bills and he manipulated these very cleverly so that those who worked for only six days received pay for eight days, at the expense of those who had worked for ten days. He carried through this operation so neatly that the Japs never suspected what he was doing. Thus all who worked for six days or more got the bonus. It says a great deal for the *esprit de corps* of our chaps that nobody ever complained that he was not receiving his full pay.

The Japanese tried to take every man who could do a day's work, however difficult he might find it, for the working parties. I never helped a fit man to avoid work, but I am not ashamed to say that I told ill men to fake symptoms to enable them to avoid reaching breaking point. It was no good telling the Japs that a man was not well; there had to be some visible proof of his disability. I would show the soldiers how to give the appearance that their hands or legs were twisted and coach them in the replies they should make to inquisitive members of the prison staff, who came inquiring into their condition.

When a large number of men were taken for working parties, those of us who were left in No. 3 Block had to bear the burden of a greatly increased number of fatigues. This we shouldered as cheerfully as possible but time was the vital factor. If we did not get the fatigues done quickly, the Japanese used to beat us up. There would have been nothing particularly difficult in the fatigues, if we had had the proper equipment to do them. As an example of what we were up against, we had to scrub the barrackroom floors twice a week with pieces of sacking, bits of coir and a bucket of dirty water. There was never enough water available to do the job properly. The room-washing was done by two people, who were expected to move the beds and kit and then wash the floor. In the upstairs rooms, the water used to leak through the wooden floor on to the verandah below.

From November, 1942, for six months, I, in addition to my medical work, shared the responsibility for this floor-washing in our barrackroom with a prison warder, named Smith, from the prison at Fort Blair in the Andamans. For six months, until April, 1943, I had this little group of men from the Andamans with me in my barrackroom. They were all civilians and at that date they were transferred into internment at Tavoy. They included the Chief Commissioner of the Andamans, a Church of England padre named Black, who was sixty-five, a Salvation Army brigadier named Francis, who was sixty, and several other prison officials. They were a plucky little band of elderly civilians and both Mr. Black and Mr. Francis took their religious responsibilities seriously, holding services, conducting funerals and discussing problems with the men.

The nominal pay for officers was quite fair, but it has to be remembered that it was calculated in the occupation rupees that the Japanese issued in Burma, a currency that had no real value—in fact, the streets of the towns of Burma were littered with these occupation rupees after the liberation. Officers' pay ranged from Rs. 41 (about £3 3s.) a week for a second lieutenant to Rs. 80 (about £6) for a brigadier or a full colonel. The Japs had a system, however, by which the pay disappeared as snow before the summer's sun. Both Hobson and I, for example, received Rs. 320 a month, on paper. From this was first deducted Rs. 200

and this sum was put into a Jap Savings Bank book in our names. We were told that all Japanese officers and men had to contribute from their pay to help the Japanese war effort and so must we! It was all done with that respect for formality that characterises the Japanese. We had to sign each month that Rs. 200 had been deposited by us in the Savings Bank.

There were two further deductions and one appropriation. We were told that officers must pay for their own food, as they were paid so generously, and Rs. 60 a month were deducted for this purpose. Then we agreed to place to the credit of the men's Messing Fund another forty rupees a month, so that they could have extras on their diet; this we did cheerfully but we did not get value for money. This left Hobson and me with fifty rupees a month apiece. We received forty and nobody bothered to tell us what had happened to the other ten!

It must be admitted that the money received by the officers and that earned by the men was very useful in providing us all with something just a little better than the eternal rice diet. In the early days, men out on the working-parties could, with the permission of the sentries, purchase for us sixteen duck or hen eggs for a rupee. They could also get eighty of the best Burmese cheroots, in packets of four, wrapped in cellophane, or 100 good cheroots for the same price. By 1945, eggs were Rs. 3 each and two indifferent cheroots cost a rupee. One did not need to be an economist to realise that the financial stability of the Great Japan was tottering.

When things became very expensive, Hobson wrote to the Commandant on two occasions and requested that the officers should be permitted to withdraw some of the money in the Savings Bank to purchase cheroots for the men. To our surprise, this was permitted and Hobson and I drew Rs. 6,100 for this purpose. We obtained receipts from the

Men's Canteen Committee for these amounts before we left Rangoon and I left mine with the Paymaster at Deolali Transit Camp, when we tried to work out the pay question on the way home.

I have mentioned working-parties frequently in this book, but I must make one or two general comments about them here. The principal victims in Rangoon Jail were the British, American and Indian prisoners there. The parties were a wicked form of slave labour. No Tippoo Sultan could have wreaked his vengeance on unfortunate prisoners of war more cruelly than the way in which the Japanese exacted day labour from our men.

The parties were sent out to work before daylight, without any breakfast, in a tropical climate. They often came back after dark to eat only a cold or tepid meal consisting principally of rice and vegetables, with perhaps a little tough meat. This they did, month after month, both in the hot season and during the monsoon.

After we had been in jail for about a year, we were given the astonishing news that the officers were to be allowed servants. These were allotted on a scale of one each for officers of the rank of brigadier and colonel, one between two lieut.-colonels, one for every three majors, and one for every four junior officers. These servants were detailed to fetch meals from the kitchens, to wash up dishes and to do the barrackroom fatigues. They were paid by the officers in money or in cheroots, eggs or other purchasable eatables. There was considerable competition for these jobs, as they had very clear advantages over coolie labour outside but the scheme did not last long.

As, owing to deaths and illness, the Japs found it more and more difficult to maintain the numbers in the working parties, they announced that the 'light-duty' men could do the work of officers' servants. This was patently absurd as the duties involved a considerable amount of hard, physical labour and many of the 'light-duty' men were suffering from scabies or ringworm or were convalescents from beri-beri.

My own servant, Private G. A. Ratcliffe of the Second Battalion of the K.O.Y.L.I., an artistic, sensitive man, was taken away from me but he was not employed on outside labour. The Commandant, himself, used his services as a landscape artist and water-colour painter. We were able to bring some of Ratcliffe's sketches, greeting-cards and regimental crests in colour out of jail with us, and some of his work is reproduced in this book.

Two things that we had to do that I found particularly irksome were to learn Japanese drill and to acquire a know-ledge of the Japanese language, particularly words of com-mand. The officers were somewhat handicapped in this endeavour, for when we emerged from 'solitary' we found that the men were fairly familiar both with the drill and the words of command. They had, when they moved off on working parties, had experience of being under Jap guards who numbered and controlled them in Japanese.

One morning, the officers were assembled in one of the barrackrooms and lined up facing a sentry and an inter-preter. We were each handed four pages of words of command in Japanese characters with their English equivalents inserted. Then started a pantomime that was repeated for several weeks. The sentry—we nicknamed him the 'Schoolmaster'—was a fat-faced, peering little Japanese, very like the diligent Jap students who could be seen scurrying around the streets of our University cities in this country before the war. He took himself very seriously and would make us repeat words in unison, as children used to do in Infants' Schools. He insisted in his fussy, dogmatic way that we must learn by heart words like: *Tenko*, roll-call; *Kiotsuke*, attention; *Keirei*, salute; *Bango*, number; and *Yasume*, stand-at-ease.

Most of us found the numbers very difficult, especially when the 'Schoolmaster' took us up into the twenties and thirties. The lesson was not made easier by the fact that, in Japanese, there are two different words for some of the numbers.

The great slogan of the Japs was: *Nippon go o manabe* (Learn the Japanese language). *Greater Asia* ran a feature under this title, which we were continually exhorted to study. The study was not made any more palatable by the form that these articles took. The first one started:

"To the readers—First and foremost, we should offer our hearty thanks to Nippon.
Second to her soldiers for their bravery and courage.
'Dear soldiers we thank you very much!'
  (*Heitaisan, arigato gozaimasu!*)
Lastly we hope that the Empire of Nippon will grow greater and greater.
'Hip, Hip, Hip, Hooray!'
  (*Banzai! Banzai! Banzai!*)"

After the English-speaking medical corporal, 'the Paper Boy', left the staff of the prison, I had an added trial. I was then forced to keep a notebook and compile a vocabulary of all Japanese medical terms and the names of things like drugs and dressings. I still have that book in which I entered much of value, including particulars of the diet of special prisoners. I must have been somewhat optimistic at times, too, for I see that I have entered there the number of my Japanese Savings Bank book, J/07847. I wonder where those savings are today!

Whenever there was a change of Jap medical staff, my senior N.C.O., Sergeant 'Kashkan' Smith and I were always looked upon with the gravest suspicion for the first few days. We made it our policy never to make any advances to newcomers, for there was always the possibility that such might be rewarded with a clout over the head. Instead, we watched warily to see whether they would make any overtures. When they did, they usually took the form of asking how old I was, a subject in which the Nips took a perennial interest. Once the ice was broken in this way, they might go on to ask if we were married and if we had any children. When we gave them this information, they would want to know the ages of our wives and children and whether we had any photographs of our families to show them. I made it my policy to ask them the same questions in return.

The Japs liked to talk about themselves and their relatives in Japan, when in a sentimental mood. They would produce photographs of their wives and offspring and also of the houses in which they lived. They would then go on to talk about Japan, the cherry-blossom trees and the chrysanthemums, about their fish, their streams and their countryside in quite a friendly sort of way. Sometimes for a few minutes it was difficult to realise that the Japs were brutal and uncivilised. We never felt that these conversations resulted in a loss of our self-respect, either in our own eyes or in those of our jailers, but they did sometimes have a tangible reward as the orderlies would give us a cigarette or a cup of sweet tea and indeed, on two or three historic occasions, we were given a packet of twenty 'looted' British cigarettes and some extra drugs and dressings.

Two phrases in Japanese, which I did learn, stood me in very good stead on many occasions. They were:

Wataksi taihin zanin desu: I am very sorry.

Watakushi wa wakaranei: I do not understand.

I doubt if I should have got away with these phrases on some occasions if I had not been a 'man of such advanced years'.

The whole of the Jap attitude was based upon the theory that they were a superior people, yet, in their own subconscious minds, they did not believe this themselves. What genius they had was not creative but imitative. This could clearly be seen in big things, like their relations to Europeans, when they were constantly hectoring and bullying and indulging in acts of calculated brutality to convince themselves, rather than the Europeans, that they were a superior race and they would assume the most un-lovable characteristics of the white man, in an effort to impress. If I had not suffered so much at their hands and seen good men suffering more, I could find it in my heart to mix pity with the contempt that I feel for the Japs. They tried so hard to gain respect and they failed so abysmally.

The average Jap guard in Rangoon regarded himself as a fair imitation of the European. What he succeeded in being was a tenth-rate caricature of a third-rate Continental comedian, giving an impression of an Englishman. All the sentries purchased cigarette-holders in Rangoon be-cause they thought that smoking cigarettes in this manner gave them the appearance of a 'pukka sahib'. The fact that they could not stomach even the mildest of British cigarettes did not prevent them from continuing this pose. They smoked de-nicotinised, Japanese cigarettes through holders!

The Nips made no effort, in the early days of our im-prisonment, to provide us with clothing. One of the first things that they did was to take away the prisoners' boots and these they wore themselves. By the end of our time in jail, they were even collecting for themselves the waist-tapes from our shorts.

We should have been even worse dressed than we were, except that members of the Burmese Assembly protested to the Japs against badly clothed, almost naked British and Indian prisoners marching through the streets of Rangoon. They said that it was a degrading spectacle, reflecting little credit upon Imperial Nippon. This was the right approach and the result was that men, who were going out on working-parties, and whose clothing was in shreds, were given shirts and vests and a pair of shoddy drill shorts.

When the rains began about the end of our first April, I risked intervening with Coshima and wrote a letter complaining about the men having to go to work every day in wet clothing. I took good care to stress the point that this procedure was leading to illness, for I knew that the most effective way of gaining a response from the Japs was to draw their attention to the fact that their policy was leading to a reduction of the number of men available for working-parties.

Coshima did not acknowledge receipt of this letter, although I was apprehensive that I might draw his anger upon my head. However, a day or two later, just before evening roll-call, we saw a bundle of undervests and khaki drill shorts being carried into the compound.

When we paraded, O'Hari San called me out of the ranks and snarled: "You wrote a letter to Captain Coshima about clothing the other day?"

"I did," I admitted.

"Well," said he, "the Quartermaster is issuing clothing, shirts and shorts today but that has nothing to do with the letter you wrote, nothing at all to do with that letter, do you understand? Do you clearly understand that?"

The interpreter cleared his throat and spat on the ground —a habit of his that I found particularly displeasing.

As the Japanese war position worsened, they were not only unwilling, but unable, to issue us with proper clothes. First they supplied us with large pieces of khaki for patching, then we descended to green Dutch drill and eventually to ordinary pieces of sacking. With these various materials, shorts and shirts were patched and patched and patched again until, often, the original garment shirt did not equal in weight the patchings.

The men out on working-parties and the cooks stole pieces of sacking and brought these into the compound and we used them for repairing blankets, and as towels.

Most of the men who went out to do coolie labour walked bare-footed but, on two occasions, the parties were issued with wooden sandals. These, however, were of the shoddiest variety and were virtually impossible to march upon. Any man who was able to use them found that they lasted for only a very short time, but that did not worry the Japs. They did not comprehend the meaning of the familiar term in the British services—'reduced to produce'. The broken remains of the sandals had to be kept in the barrack-rooms and they were frequently checked by the Japanese Quartermaster's staff. They were determined that their inventory should not be wrong!

Kit inspections were frequent but they seldom seemed to lead anywhere. The Quartermaster would inspect the prisoners at roll-call but, even when clothes were almost dropping off the backs of the men, it was only on the rarest occasions that a totally inadequate scale of replacements was issued.

Brigadier Hobson and I complained about clothing and about food, time and time again, but so little notice was taken of our letters on these subjects, that, eventually, we decided that we were wasting our time and inviting reprisals upon the other prisoners and upon ourselves.

We would have been in a sorrier plight still, if it were not for the ingenuity of some amongst us. The Japs could never understand how new made-up lengths of cloth, shirts and shorts appeared on many men, whom they were convinced only had old clothes.

The *modus operandi* that led to this amelioration of our condition was, like most clever plans, extremely simple. When the working-parties went out to Rangoon, they carried with them single bamboo poles on each of which were slung two pails of rice for a midday meal. These poles were supported on the shoulders of two prisoners in typically Asiatic fashion. The poles that were used at first were somewhat slender but they were replaced by others much larger and thicker.

One man discovered that the poles could be split almost along the whole of their length and that the cut could not be detected, provided that the split end was bound with a piece of string. Into these splits would go all the cloth that the parties were able to buy or appropriate while they were out. Our men had little conscience about taking property in Japanese-occupied territory. They knew that, if they left things, the Japs would probably commandeer them and, in any case, we had reached the frame of mind where we felt that the world owed us a living.

We struggled hard to maintain cloth, for what we considered to be a great responsibility. We tried to bury our dead with decency and to pay them what respect we could. In the early days, we were able to get blankets for this purpose; then we had to resort to pieces of sackcloth; finally the situation defeated us completely and we had to place the uncovered bodies in rough wooden boxes, fashioned by our own carpenters.

When a comrade was to be buried, we all stood at attention, after parading in the compound, while the funeral party marched past us at the slow march. The body was then carried by six of our men to the English cemetery and buried as reverently as the conditions would allow.

The Japs' attitude towards our funerals changed as the months went by. When first we had deaths, there was no cause for complaint. I have already told that the only time I left the jail was, during the first few weeks, to conduct a service on the death of my medical colleague, Captain Kilgour. The Japs then were placing a small wreath of paper flowers at the graveside. Later the Japs seemed to think that it was sufficient to throw the bodies into the ground, like those of dogs, but we fought to maintain our rights. Power was foremost in these efforts. He, as a labour of love, maintained a careful record of the deaths and would always seek an opportunity of holding a short Service, when a man died.

Our men made crosses, on which were inscribed the number, rank, name and unit of the deceased. These were placed on the graves but some ghouls removed these crosses almost as soon as they were erected. This vandalism continued throughout our imprisonment and we were never able to discover the perpetrators.

Perhaps never did our resentment against our captors blaze more fiercely than, when we stood, motionless at attention, as we paid our last tributes to our dead. In life our men suffered every possible indignity and cruelty and it was an unnecessary refinement of barbarity for them to be subjected to the mean and petty treatment that their lifeless bodies experienced as they went to their last resting places.

Bombed by our Friends

THERE is no doubt that, when we entered Rangoon Jail, the Japanese thought that they had won the war and that they were presiding over the final liquidation of the British Empire in the Far East. All the facts supported this supposition. Not only had the armies of Nippon swept aside white troops everywhere they had encountered them, but they had also succeeded in penetrating into India itself and were openly boasting that soon they would move forward from their bases in Assam, through the rich plains of Bengal, and capture Calcutta, second largest city of the British Commonwealth. As I have emphasised before, we had no facts with which to contradict their arguments or their assurance, for we were not in possession of any authentic news of the progress of the war—all that we had were the highly biased accounts that the Japs saw fit to release to us from time to time.

We were only too familiar with the highly-explosive political situation in India and could feel no confidence that the nationalist politicians there would not sabotage the Allied war effort in the misguided belief that, by so doing, they were furthering the idea of independence on which they had set their hearts. It seemed to us that, before long, it was possible that we should become just a little pocket of Europeans, situated in a vast continent, dominated by our enemies.

This was the background against which our experience of British and American bombing must be viewed. It would be mock-heroic to pretend that we welcomed the possibility of being killed by Allied bombs, in the common cause, for life was the thing that we held on to tenaciously, even when we were in circumstances that robbed us of all the zest of living. I do not think that many of us thought about it consciously but we were surely sustained by the conviction that, if we could hang on to life in the desperate circumstances in which we found ourselves, we should of a certainty be able to win through to better things.

Nevertheless, we looked upon British and American aircraft as harbingers of our ultimate release. They brought to us the unspoken message that our friends were still in the war and that the battle for civilisation was still on. Our planes might accidentally strike heavy blows upon us but, at the same time, they were inflicting intentionally upon our enemies mortal wounds.

In the very early days, it was an event to see an Allied plane. Sometimes, we would catch sight of a British or American aircraft, flying very high, on a reconnaissance mission. These sorties did not seem to worry our captors unduly. They had little A.A. protection at Rangoon at this time and, in any case, the planes were flying too high for gunfire to be operated against them successfully; neither did they seek to engage them with fighter aircraft.

We had been in Rangoon Jail for nearly a year before we experienced bombing then, and from our point of view, that bombing was about as successful as it could possibly be. A single British fighter-bomber flew over the city and dropped two bombs just beside the main gate of the prison. Three of the Japanese guards were killed. One of these was the 'Little Lance-Corporal', that fiend who acted as Coshima's right-hand man and who was always foremost in any wickedness and cruelty, indulged in by the Japs. The second was another N.C.O., whom we called, amongst ourselves, 'Pie-face'. He had not the ingenuity of the 'Little Lance-Corporal' but he was also a thoroughly bad type, disliked by us all. I remember that once he gave Power and me a good punching in the face, because we had failed to notice that he had come to lock the garden-gate and, consequently, had omitted to call our squad of officers to attention. The third victim was a private called 'Smiler', a simple, rustic fellow, who went about the prison with a grin on his yellow face and was only sadistic in so far as he had to carry out the orders of his superiors. 'Smiler' might have been quite a useful member of society, if it had not been his fate to be the servant of barbarians.

This attack was followed by reprisals on the part of the Japanese to our prisoners. Discipline was tightened up immediately and we forfeited all the small privileges we had gained for a time. We had to listen to an interminable hymn of hate from our jailers, who complained of 'indiscriminate bombing' and drew attention to the unfair way in which the British were treating the Great Japan.

This was, however, only an isolated incident and it was not until the following year that Allied planes began to appear over Rangoon in any force. Early in 1944, we saw a flight of from twenty to thirty American planes going over in swan formation and we were encouraged to see that, as a result of this, the Japs felt it necessary to increase immediately their anti-aircraft defences. From then on, Rangoon was subjected to a good deal of bombing and, in the jail, we had our share.

It was all very exciting. We would watch the searchlight beams seeking out our planes in the sky, and, when one was held, we would witness Nip fighters ascending into the light and attacking. It must be admitted that they did this with great daring and with a reckless disregard for consequences, throwing themselves in very close and drawing the accurate and relentless fire of our rear-gunners. It was Japanese policy to bring down our planes if they could, without any regard for the number of pilots or machines they lost themselves.

One frightful afternoon, the Japs succeeded in hitting an American bomber and it jettisoned its load of four five-hundred pound bombs. All of them hit the jail. One landed, comparatively harmlessly, on the wall outside the Indian Block; the second landed in the middle of the Indian compound and blew to pieces the central part of the block, killing about a dozen Indian prisoners and wounding many more. The third dropped on the old hospital kitchen of No. 3 Block—by the mercy of Providence, we had moved the hospital kitchen to the eastern corner of the compound, only a few days earlier. This bomb was only seventy feet from the southern flank of the block, where the officers' rooms were on the first floor. The last of the stick landed on the northern flank of the block, on our basket-ball pitch, ninety feet away from our barrackroom.

These bombs killed two British prisoners outright and severely wounded three others, who died later. Twelve others were injured, including myself. My right eardrum was ruptured and sixteen small pieces of bomb penetrated my right side. One, on my right temple region, resulted in my face and glasses being covered with blood, before I was able to control the haemorrhage.

This particular incident had a curious sequel. I was sitting on a box in the compound, using a broken piece of mirror, given to me by one of the men, in an endeavour to pick out some of the pieces from the back of my knee with a bamboo stick. As I worked away, the Japanese Commandant for all Rangoon, a fussy little elderly Major-General, nicknamed 'Goaty-Beard', came into the compound. I tried to get to my feet but he waved me down and to my intense surprise saluted me, saying: "I am very sorry, I am very sorry indeed." He then proceeded inside and visited the wounded, who had previously been attended to by me.

Next day, old 'Goaty-Beard' sent to Hobson two large tins of Australian skimmed milk powder and some English rolled oats in tins for the injured. I have never been able to think up an explanation of this little episode, so out of character for the Japanese, and presume that it may not have been unconnected with the fact that bombing sowed in the Japanese mind the uncomfortable idea that victory for the forces of Nippon was not inevitable.

Now, when bombing was on, I always made my way down to our No. 3 Block M.I. Room, so as to be on the spot, should casualties take place. The following evening, about nine o'clock, another bomber, obviously aiming for the junction of the Prome-Rangoon road, just outside the jail, dropped its load on No. 3 Block.

One bomb burst in the compound, where we had dug slit trenches, which were packed with prisoners. A second dropped in the garden of the block, near the high boundary wall, scarring it deeply and removing much brick and plaster. I was standing in the doorway of the M.I. Room, when the first bomb exploded, sending up a shower of bricks and dust. I saw the whole roof of the main latrine lifted off by the explosion and crash to the ground beneath.

This all happened in the pitch-dark and the absence of light handicapped our fellows in their efforts to form themselves into rescue-parties. This handicap, however, was as nothing compared to the handicap that resulted from the misguided efforts of our captors, who became quite hysterical under bombing and rushed about shouting excitedly and interfering everywhere. In the moment of crisis our rôles were reversed and we had to quieten the Japs and take command of the situation, before prison routine could be restored.

That night, we did not lose a single man through being struck by bomb-casing or high explosive but ten of our chaps were killed by blast. It might well have been more for, amongst those who recovered from this bombing, there was one man with a fractured clavicle, one with a dislocated acromial end of his collar-bone and one with severe spinal injuries.

After these incidents, the jail escaped further severe bombing, although the city of Rangoon was subjected to many heavy attacks. By 1945, heavy carpet bombing of Rangoon by Flying Fortresses and other heavy American bombers was almost a daily occurrence and we lived in an atmosphere of bombs and A.A. fire.

Looking back, it is useful to report the effect of bombing upon the Japanese. There are two schools of thought about the military effectiveness of bombing civilian targets in time of war. There can be little doubt that the German policy of bombing the towns and cities of this country fortified and strengthened the resolve of our people to prosecute the war to a successful conclusion. We were in a unique position to observe that bombing had exactly the opposite effect upon the Japanese. It inculcated fear in them and weakened their resolution.

After a heavy bombing attack, the interpreters would run about for days, mouthing slogans like: 'indiscriminate bombing', 'total war' and 'cowardly attacks'. They were always trying to persuade our officers to broadcast about bombing and, as I have already reported, they did read over their broadcasting system an essay by one of our officers in which he commented ironically upon the Japanese attitude to Allied bombing.

Our airmen cannot be blamed for bombing the jail. As we pointed out to the Japs, time and time again, we always ran the risk of being bombed, unless the prisoner-of-war camps were illuminated at night, in accordance with international law, and were clearly marked by day.

It was no credit to the Japanese that we did not suffer even worse than we did from Allied bombing.

We Did Have Some Fun

SOMETIMES, when I see a note in the newspapers nowa-days, that some well-known entertainer has visited Dartmoor or one of our other great jails to provide amuse-ment for the criminals there, I think how very much more fortunate are wrong-doers in this country than were we, who had committed no offence but who fell into the hands of the Japanese during the war. Our captors certainly did not put themselves out to provide us with entertainment!

In fact, the only time I ever remember the Japanese relaxing the austerity they imposed upon us was when, one evening in 1943, we were suddenly paraded. A remark made by O'Hari San, when he came to announce this parade, caused great excitement. He said to me: "You are very lucky, you are very lucky indeed." This observation gave rise to the wildest rumours and, within a few minutes, many of our men were convinced that we were about to be released.

It was, therefore, something of an anti-climax, when we were marched round to the Indian Block and told to sit on the ground and listen to a band performance. It was a strange scene as groups of Indian, Chinese, British and American prisoners squatted on the ground in the com-pound, with our guards sitting on chairs and wooden forms, while a Japanese band played with great enthusiasm, its conductor swinging his arms as vigorously as any band leader I have ever seen. The thoughts of us all must have turned to happier days, when we had heard similar bands, playing in more congenial circumstances. It was not a bad

Birthday Card, 1944, received by the Author from the
Cameronians

concert and it made a welcome break in routine. The best items were the playing of 'The Japanese Soldier Goes to the Front' and a selection from 'William Tell', and the xylophonist and the oboe players acquitted themselves quite creditably.

This concert was the only effort made by the Japanese during the whole time we were in jail to relieve the tedium of our imprisonment. All other recreation we had to provide ourselves and even then it was only allowed by the grace of our captors.

In 1942, on *Yasume* days, or holidays, we were permitted to hold, amongst ourselves, a concert or a sing-song. These days then took place every Thursday but the exigencies of prison life caused them later to be held at much more infrequent intervals. *Yasume* days became rarer and rarer as the men were made to work every day, for long periods on end, without a rest. Eventually, we were lucky if we could organise a concert once a month, and we had to have special permission from the Commandant to hold them.

Many of these concerts reached a high standard and the highlights were those that we held to celebrate Christmas and New Year in 1943 and 1944. Some of our fellows possessed very good voices and we got a lot of fun out of a jazz band with improvised instruments, in which the leading lights were Rifleman Laws, the late Corporal Bailey and 'Smudger' Smith. Our star turn, however, was the comedian, W.O. Richardson of the R.A.F. Richardson was a Lancashire man and could mimic Stanley Holloway and would adapt his patter to bring in the names of his fellow-prisoners in his topical songs and stories. He would never lose an opportunity of getting in a sly dig at the guards if he could do so, without their understanding what he was about. Two of his most popular acts featured references to Brigadier Hobson's bald head and shaved-off beard and a comic sick parade conducted by me. It was all done so cleverly, and with such absence of malice, that his victims derived as much amusement out of the performance as anybody else.

Richardson was one of the leading lights in our Christmas pantomimes. He, along with Corporal Caton and Lieutenant Wild, gave a tremendous amount of time and energy to the organising of these and it has to be remembered that all this time had to be 'won' from the Japanese. Men would come back from the working-parties, dog-tired at night, and would willingly sacrifice their rest so that they could prepare for the time, when they would be able to lighten the burden of their comrades for a little while at least. Quite a number of the Nip sentries were in the habit of attending our shows, especially at Christmas time.

We had a great many Scotsmen in the jail and I take particular pride in the way in which they came to regard me as their particular friend. It has been said that, wherever two Scots meet, a Caledonian Society is formed. So it was in Rangoon Jail. The Scots named me as the 'Senior Jock' and took delight in recognising me by courtesies that uplifted my heart. Using what scant materials were available, they presented to me, on special occasions, such as Christmas, the New Year and my birthday, cards of beautiful design and intricate workmanship. These cards are now amongst my most treasured possessions, and examples are reproduced in this book.

On my fifty-fifth birthday—the fourth I spent in jail—the Scots invited me to review them. This invitation I accepted with pleasure. The ceremony should have been held on 24th April, 1944 but we postponed it for a few days. The Japs were in a particularly ugly mood at this time and Brigadier Hobson and I decided that it would be more tactful to wait until we were granted a *Yasume* day. Then we would proceed with the review, holding it between the time of evening roll-call and the start of the concert.

The programme was as follows:

1. On Parade.
2. Inspection by the 'Senior Jock'.
3. Presentation of Medal.
4. Address.
5. March Past.

Foremost amongst the organisers of this event, as might have been expected, was that indomitable Scottish patriot, Piper Birse of the Cameronians. The Jocks spent every minute of their spare time for days in making Balmoral bonnets from rice-sacks. Birse presented me with one with all the aplomb of a football-pool proprietor handing out a £75,000 dividend. The men arrayed themselves in hackles of pigeon feathers, but pigeon feathers were not considered good enough for the Chief. I was given a hackle of kites' wing feathers, appropriated from the Japanese M.I. Room. I was, of course, unable to obtain a 'crummock' so instead I carried a short pole.

I thought that it would be a suitable gesture to ask two other prisoners, whose birthdays were on the same day as mine, to share the honours with me. They were Pilot Officer 'Brother' G. P. Kirwan, a South African, and Sergeant 'Sammy' Meek of the Gloucestershire Regiment. They accepted the invitations but did not put in an appearance at the parade, from the mistaken idea that they should do nothing that might take away from the glory of 'my day'.

(I should have been particularly pleased to share the day with Sergeant Meek, for his devotion to duty is something that I shall never forget. He was only a lad of 20, when he was taken prisoner but we were fortunate to have him with us, for he was enterprising, good-natured and resourceful. I have often expressed the view that by his efforts in the hospital cookhouse, he saved the lives of more men through cooking than the medical officers were able to do by their ministrations.)

The Scots marched into the compound, which we were using as a parade ground, in the finest Highland style. They wore their bonnets at a jaunty angle and some of them had home-made kilts and plaids swinging. Each man had a 'battle-axe' on his shoulder and they were led by Captain Bunten, who had in his right hand a drawn wooden sword. The men took the occasion seriously and their appearance would not have reflected any discredit upon a gatherings of the Clans at Glenfinnan.

They insisted that I should carry through the inspection properly and stood, taut at attention, while I walked along the ranks and the age-old military question was put to them: "Any complaints?". The only deviation from military discipline was that I had contrived to have a little present for each man. I felt like Father Christmas as I handed to each man an egg, a few cigarettes or a Japanese rupee note.

After the inspection was over, I went to a small table and Fusilier Drummond came forward. He had been selected by his comrades to receive a Short Service and Bad Conduct Medal. When I had pinned this on, there came the most difficult task of all. I had to address the assembly.

I confess, without shame, that I did not find this easy, for there was a lump in my throat, as I spoke. I gave a good deal of thought to what I should say and decided to concentrate upon a humorous approach, leaving a few serious words until the end. It was, I think, a happy inspiration that caused me to interpose a few words of Gaelic into the speech.

The tenor of what I said was as follows:

"I have never seen a finer body of men anywhere. You haven't a decent pair of boots or socks amongst you. As Scotsmen, you have no hose-tops, no trews and no proper kilts. You are lousy and are covered in scabies and ring-worm. I have reason to believe, however, that this is not altogether your fault.

"However, we are all looking forward and hoping that, by my next birthday, we will be out of captivity." (We actually marched out of Rangoon Jail the day after my fifty-sixth birthday, 25th April, 1945). "I hope then that we shall be able to breathe the air of our beloved land again. I must apologise to you all for having dragged you away from your native glens to participate in such an event as this, which I am sure is unique in the history of the British Army."

There was a good deal more in the same strain. It may all seem rather simple humour now but assuredly it helped to relieve the tension on us all and this contention is borne out by the fact that there were a good many wearing Balmoral bonnets that day, who came from south of the border or even from British territories overseas.

The first Christmas we were in jail, I racked my brains to think of some way in which I could assist the men to mark the occasion in a fitting manner. Towards the end of November, therefore, I submitted an application to Coshima, without, I must confess, much hope that it would be granted. I submitted humbly that I was anxious to give the officers and men in our compound a present of meat and said that, if the Commandant would give his permission for us to buy a pig, I would be glad to meet the cost, when called upon to do so.

A few days later, Coshima sent for Hobson and said: "I will give permission for MacKenzie's pig to be brought to the block. MacKenzie must pay for it as soon as it arrives."

As Christmas approached, we all awaited eagerly for the arrival of 'MacKenzie's pig'. Great was the excitement one day, when a Burman was sighted approaching the compound with an enormous porker on the end of a rope. He was accompanied by O'Hari San, grinning like a man possessed.

O'Hari announced: "The price is forty-three rupees. You will pay to me—forty-three rupees." I was glad to hand over this sum.

For two days, we had pork for both our midday and evening meals. It was a gala time. The hospital patients were given blood puddings and we were able to reduce the fat to dripping, which enabled us to make the rice more palatable by making it into fritters for several days.

When we came to buy a pig for Christmas, 1944, inflation beat us. We were only able to purchase a half-side of a small pig and that cost us two thousand five hundred rupees.

During 1945, however, we got a pig for nothing. This we called 'Handsell's' pig after Sergeant Handsell, our head cook, who was employed by the Japanese as a slaughterer of bullocks, pigs and water buffaloes. One day he went to collect our rations and was informed that a pig had died of *bempi* (constipation). Handsell was something of an opportunist and he suggested that to save the trouble of burying the pig, he would take it to our compound and ask the doctor to have a look at it. I was glad to act as veterinary officer, especially when I discovered that the cause of death was a straightforward obstruction of the bowel, caused by constipation. We reported to the Commandant that we were prepared to risk eating the animal and he agreed that we should be allowed to do so. He cautiously stipulated, however, that all the entrails should be returned to him and buried. As a result of Handsell's cleverness and enterprise, we obtained a whole pig for nothing, the market value of which, at that time, was five thousand rupees (about £375).

I have reported that books were scarce during the first few months of our stay. Eventually we were given a few books by the Japanese to form a library, which was supplemented by a score or so of books which the prisoners from the Andamans brought with them, including T. E. Lawrence's *Seven Pillars of Wisdom*, and a few volumes the working parties were able to bring in from the libraries of the former European Clubs in Rangoon. These last were sold to individual officers, who placed them at the disposal of the librarian and consequently were entitled to free library membership.

Another popular pastime was to bet when we would be released or recaptured. There were several books made upon this event but the question of whether bets taken in jail by prisoners were valid and should be honoured was never settled. Neither were the bets, which ran into thousands of rupees. When the day of liberation came, the men were far too excited to worry about pecuniary gain. Nevertheless, these bets did serve a very useful psychological purpose. They helped to pass the time and kept our attention firmly focussed upon the future, with a consequent rise in morale.

We devised many methods of passing the time collectively. We held quiz contests and bridge tournaments. We were somewhat handicapped in playing bridge by a shortage of cards and here the one pack, I did manage to preserve, was invaluable. After three years the denizens of a stokehold would have been ashamed to be seen with it in their hands!

Our own variety of the football pools was very popular. It might be thought that having no matches to form the basis of a pool would be a handicap, and so it was, but it was a handicap easily overcome by the simple device of voting upon the results of matches between particular teams. Supporters of teams like Glasgow Rangers and Sheffield Wednesday took a poor view when we voted that they had been defeated by Alloa or Carlisle United!

We had no equipment to play football or cricket or any

of the more usual sports but many of the younger men obtained exercise and enjoyment from basketball. In the early days, we had a proper ball for this game but, out of pure spite, the Japs took it away from us. Fusilier Leggatt, who assisted the Japanese cooks, then came to the rescue. He scrounged cows' stomachs from the kitchen and these, stuffed with dry grass, served the purpose very well indeed. Nobody who has not played basketball in the circumstances in which our men did can realise what an excellent game it is. There is nothing 'namby-pamby' about it, when played by vigorous young men, denied other outlets for their sporting enthusiasm.

The only other outdoor sport we were able to organise was quoits, played with horse-shoes. These were fairly easy to obtain and the game had the advantage that it could be played by young and old, by the fit and by the not-so-fit.

No account of the more pleasant side of prison life would be complete without a reference to those officers and men who did most to maintain our spirits. There are few who were with me in Rangoon Jail of whom I would not like to make special mention. It is a remarkable thing that, in the circumstances in which we were placed, practically all the men stood firm; only a handful let down the side and they were actuated by neurasthenia rather than by malice.

There were many times when I was only sustained by the courage, the fortitude and the cheerfulness of my comrades. Things often looked black to me, when the hospital was full and men were dying around me of beri-beri, but a courageous word from somebody even worse placed than I was never failed to encourage me.

When I was in our own hospital with beri-beri, soldiers would come to my bed before they went out to work in the morning and again in the evening, after having been out in the sun and the heat, or the rain and the mud, all day and would ask how I was. They would give me their version of the day's events and would shyly hand over a little parcel, containing perhaps a sweet potato, some carrots, a few spring onions or maybe a banana or a tomato and would gruffly say: "If that is any good to you, Sir, I'll take it down to the kitchen to be cooked for you." I did not feel then that my thanks were adequate and, even now, I know no words that can properly express my feelings.

When I was wounded and struggling, after I had been injured in the Air Raid, fellows would come up and ask me how my wounds were getting on, and ill and tired men would offer to bring things upstairs, so that I could be saved going up and down so often, and thus have a chance of resting.

It was the same when I was ordered into No. 6 Block Hospital by the Jap Commandant in 1944. Their care and interest never flagged. They never allowed their personal troubles—and, God knows, the poor fellows had enough of them—to prevent them from showing concern for their elderly Senior Medical Officer. Corporal Tweedie would send in a handful of germinated bean shoots to be cooked for me. Sergeant Handsell would bring across a piece of liver or kidney, that was his *bakshi* for slaughtering bullocks or pigs and give it to me. The cooks, when oil and fat was almost unobtainable, would come and get my egg and insist upon frying it, as they thought it would do me more good that way than hard-boiled.

Some of my good companions I have mentioned in the course of this narrative and the names of others run through my mind, like a refrain. Leggatt, Bell, Sergeant Martin, 'Skeeter' Jones, Major Ramsay, Garvin, Sergeant McKenna, 'Cushy' Mason, Ted Horton, 'Ginger' Clarkson, 'Kashan' Smith, 'Turkey' Smith, 'Smudger' Smith, 'Nobby' Clark, 'Topper' Brown, Colonel Power, Mitchell, Fern, Bryson, 'Little Albert' Hull, Golding, Yates and Bonner. I could go no like this for a long time, for to me there is music in those names but let it suffice to say that those men of the R.A.F., the Cameronians, the Gloucesters, the Koylies, the Dukes, the Lancashire Fusiliers, the Indian Army and of those regiments that were less numerously represented in our midst are for ever in my thoughts and are remembered with gratitude.

As good an example as any of the kind of men with whom I served in Rangoon Jail was Private Golding of the Thirteenth King's Liverpools. Golding came amongst us in early 1944. He had been wounded in the left eye by a bullet, before capture. He was never admitted to a hospital but only received perfunctory eye-washes from the Japanese. When he arrived in the jail, weeks after capture, his eye was still discharging and he had lost permanently his sight on the left side. As soon as he entered jail, he volunteered for the filthy work of the latrine squad and stuck to this duty, for which there was no extra pay, until the liberation.

Golding was frequently beaten up by the Jap guards for not saluting, for they made no allowance for the fact that he could not see them coming on one side. He never complained and maintained a cheerful outlook, even when he could hardly stand, after ill-treatment. His unassuming manner and his willingness to tackle the dirtiest work with good humour and thoroughness was an example to us all and he did much to maintain the morale of his fellow prisoners.

Liberty—At Last

IN the early weeks of 1945, we missed some of the familiar faces amongst the prison staff. We were glad to hear that they had been medically examined and sent off to the front. We were delighted to see the last of them and we regarded their departure as a good omen, for we knew that, if the Japs were reduced to using some of that material as fighting troops, they must be in a bad way indeed.

What guards were left were more friendly and we were given better food. The working-parties reported that Indians and Burmese in the streets were throwing money, cheroots and fruit to our men in the streets and calling out: "It won't be long now."

On 17th April, 1945, we realised that the Japs were on the retreat. On that date, seventeen Jap fighters took off from the airfield at Mingaladon, circled Rangoon quite close to the jail and, after doing a sort of 'Victory Roll', flew away towards Japan. For months previously, we had hardly seen a Japanese plane and we were comforted by the reflection that the Allies must have gained complete air supremacy in the skies over Burma, for British and American fighters were being allowed to escort our bombers on their missions, quite unimpeded. Nearly every day, there was dive-bombing on the city and we could hear low-level fighter sweeps in the distance.

We could not help observing that the Nips in the jail were, what O'Hari San would have called: 'Very busy, very busy indeed.' They seldom came into the compound and, when the sentries did their rounds, they hurried past in a perfunctory fashion—unless they noticed something which they disliked, when they were not uninterested enough to refrain from administering a sharp beating-up on the spot.

The Japs tried to bluff us into believing that all was well but, in spite of the absence of authentic news of what was happening on the battle fronts, some sixth sense told us that we were on the eve of a great crisis. We felt that the end was very near.

It was an exciting time but, in some ways, it was a terrifying time too. We could not be sure that the Japs would not panic and perhaps carry through a massacre. Many of the Japanese with whom we came into contact were hardly sane by European standards and it was impossible to predict what they would do under the strain of a dire emergency.

At first, it seemed certain that our captors were determined to hold on to Rangoon, if it was at all possible. They seemed to be preparing for a siege. Corporal Tweedie and his *moashi* boys were told to close down the bean-germinating plant. It was regarded as an unnecessary frill. The stores in the jail canteen were sold to inhabitants of Rangoon and no replacements came in for them. Pigs, bullocks and water buffaloes were slaughtered recklessly. The working parties reported that sheds and buildings all over Rangoon were being commandeered to hold stocks of rice, potatoes, onions and *juggaree*. These provisions were being brought into the city in barges and on trains and our men had the job of unloading them and stacking the bags in the improvised storehouses.

Towards the end of March, an incident occurred that showed that we were most certainly not out of the wood. Some of our men on jail fatigues discovered a box in one of the solitary cells near the guardroom. They prised it open and found that it was full of cakes of very good soap. It was the first soap that many of us had seen for a long time

A Group of Prisoners 'unfit to march' taken at Rangoon Jail after the Liberation

The Author (with beard) tells his story at Advance H.Q., 224 Group—Neville Shute on right

and the finders found many willing purchasers, with no questions asked. It was a sign of the change in the jail atmosphere that many of our chaps did not think it necessary to be as careful as they would have been previously to hide their soap. When the Jap guards found that the box had been rifled the fat was in the fire.

A sentry, one morning, came into one of the officers' barrackrooms, looked round, picked up two or three pieces of this soap and dashed off to the guardroom with them. News of this spread round the compound like wildfire. Prisoners could be seen, hiding the soap everywhere with frenzied speed. They threw it up the trees, they buried it in the garden, they stowed it in the roof and they placed it on the cooks' fire. Everything was done as quickly as possible, for we knew that a search would be instituted within a few minutes. The quickness of the operation was our undoing. When the jailers rushed over to No. 3 Block to begin their search, there was still soap in the barrackrooms and a long series of explanations followed in an effort by the Japs to obtain an explanation for the presence of each individual cake.

Eventually Lance-Corporal Hawkins was made the scapegoat. He was forced to admit that he had stolen five pieces of soap. He was marched off to the guardroom and received a terrible thrashing. Then the Japs demanded that he gave evidence against other prisoners. This brave man stood his ground and refused to say a word. He was placed in a cell and was visited at hourly intervals during the day and night by guards who tried to force information out of him. During the waiting period, our thoughts were never far away from Hawkins, for we knew that, if the Nips could break down his resistance, the affair would have the most serious repercussions for us all. Hawkins held on and then we saw Brigadier Hobson being taken down to the guardhouse for interrogation.

Once Hawkins left us, we decided that every piece of soap in the block must be burnt. All that had been hidden was gathered in and thrown on the kitchen fire. We were only just in time, for we had anticipated, by a few minutes, a second search that covered the whole block, as with a toothcomb. At intervals over four days, our kit was ransacked and every corner of the garden and the compound was investigated. Then we had a piece of uncovenanted good fortune. We heard that some of the Nips had been found with similar pieces of soap in their possession. The hysterical agitation died down somewhat, for it was clear that all the blame could not now be laid at our door. Hawkins was returned to us, something of a hero—and rightly so. Thus ended the last of the Japanese persecutions in Rangoon Jail.

On 21st April, 1945, our prisoners, working in the Quartermaster's Store, were ordered to make up rations for five days for two hundred men. They were told to divide these rations into four consignments—each for fifty men. For this purpose, they were permitted to draw upon Japanese field rations.

At the same time, all the British and American prisoners were told that they were to be put into one of two categories. They were either 'fit to march' or 'unfit to march'. This classification was left to the senior officers amongst the prisoners. We tried to muster as many as possible in the 'fit' category, for the men were anxious to stick together and nobody who could move wished to face the unknown in a deserted Rangoon Jail. To make this possible, we inserted a third classification, or rather a sub-classification, amongst the 'fit'. We placed there one hundred men, under the command of Major Loring, who were only able to tackle light duty. The 'unfit to march', consequently, consisted of hospital cases and hopeless cripples, through sores and wounds. We gave the most careful consideration to these lists and it was, therefore, mortifying, when they were submitted to the Japanese, to have them returned immediately for alteration. There appeared to be no reason for this, except sheer pig-headedness.

We asked what we should do about medical officers and received the reply that this matter would be arranged for us. Eventually, Major McLeod was detailed to stay with the sick, and Ramsay and I were told that we were to remain on the strength of the marching party.

The Japs did take a considerable time to get the arrangements sorted out but, finally, they decided to transfer fifty of the men of Loring's party to McLeod, to act as general duty men for the sick. These fifty were placed under the charge of C.S.M. Finnerty and were transferred to No. 6 Block, which now became the headquarters of the unfit. One hundred men, under Power, were detailed as loading and dragging parties, on the line of march.

We saw that the Japanese medical staff were burning the medical records in the M.I. hut. Clearly they did not want to leave any evidence of their conduct in matters medical. While this was going on, Power's men were given the task of loading the rations on wooden handcarts and were divided into parties of five, each party being responsible for keeping one handcart on the move.

By the time these preliminaries were completed it was 25th April and, on that day, we were all issued with Japanese kit. Each man was given a soft cap, a pair of long white pants, some rubber shoes and a pair of khaki shorts. There were not enough shirts to go round and only some received one. Then each prisoner was presented with a cake of soap, and a ration bag, containing biscuits and *juggaree*, was issued to every third man. The fifty men left in Loring's party were told that their duty was to act as guards and reliefs for the handcart men.

We had no means of carrying anything on our persons

and so we tied up our pathetic little stores of belongings and carried them between us on bamboo poles. At four-thirty in the afternoon of that day, we were paraded outside the main verandah of No. 3 Block and then marched down to the guardroom. We realised that, whatever might befall us, we were about to leave Rangoon Jail. Our destination was shrouded in mystery. It was many weeks later that I learnt that the Japs in desperation had decided to make us march, through Siam, into Japan.

At last the order to set off was given. We must have looked more like an army of tramps than soldiers, as we moved out, round the outside wall on the jail and on to the Rangoon-Pegu road. There was a strong Japanese advance party at the head of our strange cavalcade and armed sentries marched alongside us. Groups of Indians and Burmese stood curiously on the side of the road, as we plodded along and greeted us with friendly grins.

I had no time to observe the scenery or our surroundings. I found that I had to concentrate on the task in hand, keeping going. In nearly three years, I had only been outside the walls of the jail once and that was in a car to attend Kilgour's funeral. I was a sick man and I was not used to walking. In fact, I do not think that I had walked more than a quarter of a mile at one stretch the whole time I was in Rangoon Jail. Neither was I used to footwear, for this was the first time that I had had shoes or stockings on my feet for a period of nearly a thousand days. Lieutenant Gover and I shared a pole and I marched grimly on through the night, able to think of little else except the need to get one foot in front of the other.

As day broke, we were called to a halt at the side of the road and allowed to rest—carts and men drawing into the jungle scrub, to avoid attracting the attention of Allied aircraft.

The Japs were pushing us hard. Before midday, we were

on the march again. Now I was feeling the effects of the unaccustomed walking along the metalled roads very much indeed. Every part of my body seemed to be aching and the weight of the pole on my shoulder was almost more than I could bear. I must have looked in bad shape, for a Japanese guard came up to me and took away my bundle and placed it on a handcart. I did not know the man, or at least, in my condition, I could not recognise him, but he did me a good turn indeed that afternoon. Later, I made out the familiar features of O'Hari San, when he came down with a message that the Commandant had given permission for the baggage of Hobson and myself to stay on the handcarts throughout the march.

It was a weird experience that second day. Sometimes, I could discern quite clearly what was going on around me; at other times, I was like a man in a fog. All the time, I kept repeating to myself: "I must keep going, I must keep going." Towards the end of that day's march, I noticed a lieutenant, who had spent most of his time in the prison hospital with a septic injury on one of his shins, reeling and staggering in front of me. Two of his comrades were trying to help him along but he finally collapsed. We were passing through a village at the time and the Japs ordered him to be left at the roadside. They said they would come back for him later, but we never saw him again. This was a pathetic case, for I had selected this officer to remain with McLeod, but he had insisted on coming with us, although he was told quite frankly that he was unlikely to survive a gruelling march.

During that second day, I was helped by a stick that Sergeant Farrar gave me. But even then, before a halt was ordered, I had come to the end of my tether. I had to resort to the device of holding on to one of the handcarts, to enable me to keep on the move. Then a surprising thing happened, along came one of the most objectionable and bumptious of our guards, a little cock of a sergeant whom we had nicknamed 'Pompous Percy' and he ordered that I should be lifted on to one of the handcarts. I finished the day being pulled along still in a daze.

I have little recollection of what happened on the third day's march. I was on the handcart all the time. We were now being harassed by Allied planes, however, and the convoy had to take cover on several occasions. Light bombs dropped all around but nobody was injured.

At day break on 28th April, we found ourselves among a few deserted Burmese huts, sheltered among thin jungle growth. Our carts had to be left standing at the roadside. Every twenty minutes or so, our fighter-bombers flew over, flying low and making it quite impossible for us to move out into the open. There is nothing remarkable in the fact that our pilots thought we were Japanese soldiers, for it has to be remembered that we were now all dressed like our captors. As a result of this Allied activity, it was impossible for us to have any food cooked that day.

We spent the day lightening our load. I only retained my haversack on a sling and put a few pieces of *juggaree* in one pocket and a number of small raw onions in the other. By this time my feet, ankles and legs were very swollen and my shoes and stockings, which I had not removed since I left Rangoon, were in shreds.

At six o'clock in the evening of that day, we prepared to move again and it came as a shock to me to hear that the Japanese had given orders that the handcarts were to be abandoned. We were approaching Pegu. Several of our party were missing by now. They had taken the opportunity to make off into the jungle. Our escort did not seem to worry unduly about the absentees.

I knew that I could not carry on for long unaided but I drew upon all my reserves of strength and determination and took my place in the line of march. Every movement

was a conscious effort but I managed to keep going until
we were called to a halt beyond Pegu. We proceeded
along the railroad track and, on either side, we saw that
demolition charges had been fixed. The mines nearer to
Wau were already wired but those on the Rangoon side
were unfilled.

I had lost all sensation in my feet. I kept knocking my
toes against stones and against the sleepers and I found it
increasingly impossible to lift my knees in a last effort
to maintain my position with my comrades. When we
halted, I knew it was all up. I sank to the ground and sent a
message up to Hobson, telling him that I was unable to
walk a step further, that my legs and feet had given way
completely. I told him that I should have to be left behind.

Nothing more was said until the end of the halt. I
rather expected some of my friends to come and say good-
bye but nobody did so. When the order to move again was
given, I just lay still, relieved to think that it was now all
over and that I should not need to renew the struggle. I
remember thinking that it was the irony of fate that I,
who had seen so much beri-beri, should fall a victim to the
results of this disease at the last lap of our adventure.

But it was not to work out that way. Just as the convoy
was moving off, Squadron-Leader Duckenfield and Captain
Brown of the K.O.Y.L.I. came up to me silently, placed
my arms around their shoulders and struggled forward,
bearing my inert body between them. Brown tried to get
me across his back after a time, but this proved too much
for him on the rough ground and in his weakened condition. They were not able to help me for long but, when
they faltered, their places were taken by other men. We
stopped every hour and at the end of each resting period,
there were always two men beside me to drag me along and
to speak a few words of comfort and good cheer.

For the last two hours the burden was borne by

Sergeants Handsell and Martin. They did more for me, as did the others, than any man had any reasonable right to expect. They had had no food themselves for forty-eight hours and they were in a distressed condition. Most of the time I was in a state of coma. In a lucid moment I asked Handsell if I had talked a lot. He confirmed that I was in a state of delirium most of the time.

These two stalwarts were with me, when we halted about seven o'clock on the morning of 29th April at a small village on the Pegu-Wau road. Here I asked O'Hari San if I could have an interview with the Jap Commandant for I had come to my decision. O'Hari asked me why I wanted to see the Commandant. I replied that it was a personal matter but when he announced that he was not prepared to forward my request, unless given a reason, I was too weary to argue any further. I drew upon my reserves and said:

"Please, O'Hari San, get the Commandant. I am finished. I cannot march any further. My legs and feet are useless and I am impeding the progress of my friends. I have disposed of my kit and, before we leave here tonight, I want the Commandant to do me a personal favour. I want him to put a bullet through my heart. I will mark the place on my shirt with a piece of paper or mark my chest with a coloured pencil, so that there will be no mistake. I cannot face being left behind to be murdered. The sooner the better, Mr. O'Hari, please, so that I may be buried before the column moves off again."

O'Hari appeared stunned and called around him a group of Japanese N.C.Os. They jabbered away amongst themselves excitedly but nobody made any move to fetch the Commandant. The next thing I knew was that Brigadier Hobson was called up to speak with the Commandant. When he went, I lay under a banyan tree—not caring much what happened now.

Within half an hour Brigadier Hobson called out to our

bewildered assembly of nearly four hundred Allied prisoners:
"We are free, we are free!"

I lay there unable to take in the news and was almost
instantaneously surrounded by thirty or forty N.C.Os. and
men shouting: "You've made it", "Congratulations, Sir",
or "Well done, Colonel, well done".

I could not speak but I held my hand out feebly and one
by one my companions ran up and shook it. It was perhaps the proudest moment of my life. It made me realise
that what little I had been able to do for these splendid
fellows in the way of doctoring and by being, as far as I
could, their guide, philosopher and friend was deeply
appreciated. What better tribute could any man wish from
his companions in adversity?

It soon got round that the Jap Commandant had told
Hobson that he had decided that the march must be
abandoned and that he had decided that he and his men must
return to Rangoon. They were giving up responsibility for
the prisoners and passing over command to Hobson.
Within a few minutes, the Japs marched quickly away from
us. We noticed that they were moving in the opposite
direction to Rangoon!

That day was spent in obtaining food from the Burmese
villages in the neighbourhood and it was supplied against
promises that we would pay for it when we reached our own
lines. The members of the R.A.F., under Duckenfield,
employed themselves in making a huge Union Jack from
pieces of cloth that the Burmans gave them and from the
long white pants with which the Japs had issued us.

Hobson took over a Burmese rush hut in the village as
an office and I was helped over to a small room, that was
above his office. There I lay, reflecting on a bare wooden
bedstead when shouts warned us that there were Allied
aircraft overhead. Hobson rushed to my side and said:
"What are you going to do, Mac?"

I replied: "I don't think there is much time," so he pulled and lifted me on to the floor and then lay down beside me. He lay on his side with his hand and forearm on my thigh.

A forty-three pound bomb exploded just behind the hut, sending bomb splinters and pieces of the structure flying in all directions. Neither of us was hurt.

"My God, that was a near one," I heard Hobson say.

"I don't think it's all over yet," was my reply.

Then the aircraft began to machine-gun us. The first bullet from the left hand gun hit Hobson, squarely in the right kidney region and inflicted a deep wound about two inches long. I felt the concussion as it was communicated to me through his hand and forearm.

The first bullet from the right hand gun passed by my ear and lodged itself in the junction of the wall and floor in front of me. I could hear it singing, as it passed. Had I been leaning on my elbow, as I usually did on such occasions, when lying on the ground, I would not be alive today.

I turned round, as I was unable to use my feet and legs, and took out a small piece of Japanese adhesive plaster from my pocket, looking at the same time for Hobson's wound. A glance told me that adhesive plaster was no good. Blood was pouring from the wound and Brigadier Hobson was dead.

Poor Hobson! Could anything be more poignant? He was destroyed by our own side, after the years he had suffered at the hands of the enemy. Yet, I am not sure that, if he had to go, he would not have wished it that way. He died in the moment of his triumph for surely it was his finest hour, shortly before, when he stood in front of us, waving a piece of paper and announcing to us all: "We are free."

I straightened his body out, as best I could, and called to two men sheltering below, to give me a hand and to find Captain Harvey, who had succeeded Colgan as our adjutant.

When Harvey came in, I told him what had happened and suggested that we had better leave Hobson where he was, until we could get an opportunity of burying him, when the danger of air raids was over.

Harvey and the others assisted me down the stairs and over to a large tree by the railway line. We selected a site on the other side of the railway and W.O. Richardson and a party started to dig a grave.

If the aircraft had come over a few minutes later, we might well have been spared the final disaster of Hobson's death, for Duckenfield and his men had ready their Union Jack and had also prepared from white pieces of cloth a massive notice: FOUR HUNDRED BRITISH PRISONERS HERE. NO FOOD. S O S. These were now spread out on the ground and four men stood near each corner with bits of mirror in their hands to attract the attention of any Allied pilots coming over.

Our message was picked-out by a Spitfire pilot, who pin-pointed our position on his map and informed the nearest Brigade headquarters by wireless.

Towards dusk, Major Lutz, an American Mustang pilot, and one of our sergeants contacted a Burmese with a Chinese boy who had been sent out by our people to try and locate us, near the spot where the S O S had been spread out. Lutz, dressing himself in Burmese kit, accompanied the two messengers and thus found the relief-party.

After the air-raid, we decided to move our column to a village nearer Pegu on the railway, where it was possible to find food and which was large enough to accommodate us for the night. To prevent drawing attention to ourselves, with the consequent risk of air-attack, we moved off in parties of three or four. I waited behind with Captain Western and Captain Henstock and conducted a short funeral service for Brigadier Hobson. I was then helped down by them to our new headquarters, and we established ourselves there in a *pongyii*. Here we had some tea with Power and other senior officers. I was so tired and my feet were so swollen that I could not take off my shoes to enter the holy place, but the chief priest was sympathetic and urged me to make myself as comfortable as I could, as I was.

We were preparing to lie down for the night, when Major Lutz returned with the good news that he had made contact with our troops. He urged all who were fit enough to accompany him on a short cross-country journey. He persuaded me to come with them and intimated that he had arranged for the Officer Commanding, No. 37 Field Ambulance to have an ambulance waiting a short distance up the road to take me to an A.D.S.

I felt better for my rest and decided to make a last supreme effort. I had to be supported along but I did so much want to be with the main body of the prisoners when they rejoined their own side. I was half-dragged and half-lifted until we reached a number of lorries and an ambulance, parked at the side of the road.

No time was lost in lifting me up on a stretcher into the ambulance and Major Lutz and Captains Henstock and Western climbed in beside me and sat on the other side. The lorries quickly filled with excited, cheering officers and men and we started off on our journey. Within a short time the ambulance broke down! It had to be towed the rest of the way by one of the lorries. It was not a comfortable journey. We had to travel across paddy fields and irrigation banks to get to our destination and that did not make for smooth travelling. Nobody minded very much for we felt that we were already half-way back home.

Nobody that is, except Western. He was shot over the tailboard of the ambulance and, after he had picked himself up, had to be dragged back into the vehicle by Lutz and Henstock, while we were on the move. The ambulance driver knew that we wanted to stop by the shouts, but then the motive power was not under the control of the ambulance driver.

It mattered little on release night but I was tossed eighteen inches into the air and came down on the wooden edge of the stretcher, breaking a rib. My bones had become very brittle through starvation and beri-beri.

When we arrived, I was taken into the casualty clearing section of the A.D.S. and saw Major Uttam Singh Siddhu who was second-in-command of one of the Field Ambulances of our original 17th Indian Division. He was beside himself with delight to see me again and, salaaming, greeted me in characteristic Sikh fashion: "But, O Sahib, Sahib! I *am* glad to see you." He cut off swiftly what remained of my shoes and stockings and cleansed and dressed my bruised and swollen feet, then bandaged them. After he had given me a bottle of beer, some bully beef, biscuits, butter, cheese and jam, I was carried off on a stretcher to his own tent and put into a comfortable bed.

I must have slept like the dead that night. Perhaps I was given something to make me do so, for I failed to hear the firing of the Jap snipers, who were carrying on lone warfare against the tented area from surrounding houses. Uttam Singh had to get up during the night, so near was the firing.

My first visitor next day was the Field Ambulance Commander, a fellow Scot, Lieut.-Colonel A. Burns, R.A.M.C. He gave me a pair of the new jungle green battle-dress trousers that the British Army had adopted to help in jungle warfare. I was also presented with toilet requisites and a bag of Red Cross gifts. Thus accoutred, I was taken over to a site, near an airstrip, which was to be the new ambulance headquarters. I sat there in a deck chair, talking to officers and men until lunch time, watching parties clearing the area of booby traps and above all drinking in the fact that I was once again a free man.

Lunch over, Burns took me in his jeep to the air-strip, where we were to emplane for Akyab or Comilla. I suggested to Burns that he might pass the time and give some pleasure by going over to talk to the Jocks who had been prisoners with me. As he walked away, I waved to them and then settled down with my feet up to enjoy the sunshine. I was getting a good deal of amusement out of the way Burns was gesticulating to emphasise every point, when I was alarmed to see the whole party rushing for cover.

I could see nothing from my position in the car but thought that Jap planes might be approaching. I resigned myself to wait, for there was nothing else that I could do, as I was unable to move without assistance. I heard the hum of a plane and, a few seconds later, saw one descending towards the strip. When I saw that it belonged to the R.A.F., I was not unduly worried although it seemed to me a strange thing that he did not lower the undercarriage. The pilot landed on the opposite side of the strip, a narrow piece of flat ground, cut out of the jungle quite unlike an aerodrome in Britain, swayed from side to side and skidded on his wings straight for my jeep. When he was within a few yards, the plane overturned and out came the pilot from underneath the wreckage, quite jauntily, with his harness swung over his shoulder. He called out cheerfully: "I think that I ought to congratulate you on your escape, for my machine was quite out of control." I laughed with him and replied: "I think it is I that ought to congratulate *you*."

That alarm over, a Dakota landed a few minutes later and it was not long before I was airborne for Akyab, where Werhner and I spent the night in an R.A.F. hospital. Werhner's feet had given out on him by this time too.

Next morning, 1st May, 1945, I found that my services were in great demand. I was interviewed by the Public Relations Department, was photographed and talked to

British troops and Intelligence about our experiences. It was a crowded morning and, after lunch, I was busier still, for I was given a Beechcraft machine all to myself and flown to Calcutta.

We landed at Barrackpore and what a contrast there was between Calcutta, busiest city of the East, that legendary city of jute, where mingle in the streets the richest and the poorest men in the world, where fantastic and unbelievable extravagance walk hand in hand with the direst poverty and famine, and the unrelieved squalidness in which I had lived for more than three years. Calcutta has provided the highlights of leave periods for many generations of British servicemen in India but Calcutta was not for me then.

Instead I was met at the airfield by a medical officer of the R.A.F., who drove me in an ambulance to No. 21 British General Hospital, where I was lodged in the officers' wing. There began my treatment for the effects of beri-beri, consisting of two 2 c.c. injections of Vitamin B, twice daily, quantities of Marmite and Vegamite, fresh milk, cheese, eggs and fruit juice, with Vitamin B tablets. The injections continued for twenty days.

How glad I was when that finished. My abdominal wall was like a dart-board. Nevertheless, I felt fitter every day— only my eyesight lagged behind. I was, however, given a strong pair of glasses in Calcutta and was able to read the daily papers. What a treat it was to read a great newspaper like the *Statesman* of Calcutta, with its sustained reputation for objective reporting and comment, after having to put up with *Greater Asia*, or nothing at all, for three years.

Those glasses opened a new world for me. I had not realised how bad my eyesight had become, for the deterioration had set in gradually. Even the fact that I had had to stop playing bridge some eighteen months previously because I was unable to discern the markings on the cards had not brought home the fact to me that I was almost blind. I could get about and do my work and that brought to me satisfaction. In the misery in which we all lived, there was little time to give consideration to one's personal infirmities.

And so homeward-bound at last—from Calcutta to Delhi, then to Jubbulpore, Deolali and on to Poona. From here the very Dakota that had carried us to freedom conveyed me to Merryfield in the peaceful county of Somerset. I was back home in the Old Country, after an absence of five years and nine months. And what a welcome she gave me—even the Customs officials made it sweeter still by refusing to examine the luggage of repatriated prisoners of war.

Rangoon Jail from the Air after the Japanese Surrender

The Author Deputising for Mrs. MacKenzie in the Inverness W.V.S.

Postscript

I HAVE now been back in this country for nine years and, if this book had been written earlier, it would have come before the public, not as the objective statement of fact I have tried to make it, but as the vehicle of the white-hot anger of a bitter and ill-used man. Now, while I make no claim for it as a literary work, I believe that it is a plain record of the history of a single prisoner in the hands of the Japanese—a record that deserves publication because I have been fortunate enough to be able to spare the time to think things over.

I have waited with impatience for an abler pen than mine to tell the story. I have read avidly anything that has been published about the thousands of British, American, Dutch, Indian and Chinese prisoners in Burmese jails but I have found nothing that seems to convey the picture in the way that I am anxious that it should be conveyed. This is a simple, straightforward effort and it comes at a time when those who did not suffer, as my companions and I were made to suffer, are inclined to take the attitude that the time has come to allow bygones to be bygones. Perhaps this work of mine will cause some to think again. If so, I shall be well satisfied.

I am now a town councillor of the Royal Burgh of Inverness and I try to be as unlike the retired Colonel of fiction as possible. Yet every day my contempt for and hatred of the Japanese continues, if it does not increase. But now, it is a controlled contempt, a reasoned hatred, for I can see things in their proper perspective.

My mind dwells often on the march-out and on the men who were left behind, too weak through ill-treatment even to walk. I cannot sanction trade with the men who murdered my companions. I am glad to report that those who stayed behind with McLeod reached safety as we did, for they were liberated when the British troops swept into Rangoon, accompanied by Colonel Loganathan, now again, after his spell in the Indian National Army, a supporter of British rule. The lives of those men were saved but, if liberation had been postponed for another year, most of them would have died and many more of my companions and I might have died with them.

I realise that the capital on which our civilisation is living is running short. God forbid that war should come again but, if it does, it will be uncontrolled to an extent that we cannot even imagine, unless international law, The Laws and Usages of War and the Geneva Convention are strengthened and revised. Punishments for infringements must be enormously increased and agreement on this point reached by every nation in the world.

What folly it is to find that Japanese war criminals are today treated as though they were popular heroes. Soft soap by General McArthur cannot alter the facts of the case.

Let me finish by quoting reports from the British House of Commons, for when these matters were discussed then, the House was able to concentrate exclusively on the crimes that were being committed against humanity.

On 28th January, 1944, Mr. Anthony Eden (then Secretary of State for Foreign Affairs) made in the House of Commons a statement concerning Japanese treatment of British P.O.Ws. in the Far East. It was a delayed statement for it was considered to be so grave that the Government held it for a time to allow every possible check upon the authenticity of the reports upon which it was based. The announcement was made simultaneously in London and Washington. Mr. Eden referred to reports of prisoners in an "emaciated state" and went on to say that they were:

"compelled to live in tropical jungle conditions without adequate shelter, clothing, food or medical attention. Our information is that their health is rapidly deteriorating and that a high percentage are seriously ill, and that there have been some thousands of deaths."

Sir John Wardlaw Milne, Member of Parliament for Kidderminster, then added:

"The story to which the House has listened is so terrible as to make it difficult even to ask questions about it. I am certain that the Government has done everything possible to make representations to the Japanese in the ways normally open to them. Would it be possible for the American Government and ours to give notice to the Japanese that every atrocity that has taken place will be remembered and that they will be brought to account for them?"

Mr. Eden replied by saying that every representation had been tried and went on: "We have met not only with refusal but even with cynical refusal."

On 19th December in the same year, Sir James Grigg, the Secretary of State for War, reported on the position of prisoners in Japanese hands and said:

"It is a matter of profound regret to me that these disclosures have to be made; but we are convinced that it is necessary that the Japanese should know that we know how they are behaving and that we intend to hold them responsible."

I draw attention to those quotations now because there appears to be the gravest danger that the atrocities of the Japanese nation are coming to be regarded as mild misdemeanours, that can be conveniently ignored to meet the exigencies of an admittedly difficult international political situation. Those of us who were held prisoner by the

Japanese can never look upon the position in that light. We understand the nature of the beast too well. We know what was our lot and we realise that our fellow-prisoners in other camps fared no better, for did not Admiral, the Earl Mountbatten of Burma report on the work of evacuation of P.O.Ws. and civilian internees from South-East Asia: "From my own experience I can speak as to the deplorable and pitiable conditions in which we found them?"

These things need to be remembered. It was difficult enough to convince people, who wanted to believe otherwise, that in the years before 1939, the German Nazis and the Japanese fascists constituted a menace to our way of life. Today it seems to me equally difficult to bring home to a peace-loving folk that those of us who lived at the mercy of the Japanese for years found them ruthless, wicked and cruel and that their minds were possessed with dreams of ultimate world domination. I wish to sound no hysterical note about a 'Yellow Peril' but I do implore men of good-will everywhere to consider the facts and, when they have done so, to ask themselves the question: "Are we sure that the Japanese are now as democratic as they claim to be and have they indeed been converted to a belief in international co-operation and fundamental human rights?" If they have, it is certainly the quickest, the most remarkable and the most unexpected change of outlook in the history of the world.

Appendix I

A. RULES FOR PRISONERS OF WAR

1. All officer prisoners must salute all Nippon N.C.Os. (including the *Hecho* on duty and soldiers in charge of working parties), the guard commander and those who are superior to them.

2. The prisoners who are N.C.Os., or who are inferior to N.C.Os. in rank, must salute Nippon soldiers.

3. The method and action of saluting and word of command must be in accordance with Nippon Army Orders.

4. All prisoners or work parties must be escorted at all times by a Nippon soldier.

5. Should any unusual event occur or any patient be found among prisoners, it must be reported immediately to the Nippon authority, so that an instant order can be given.

6. The settled timetable must be strictly adhered to.

7. The rules concerning sanitation, which have been issued separately, must be strictly adhered to.

B. SANITATION AND HYGIENE

1. All rooms to be cleaned daily inside and outside.

2. On Sundays all bedding and clothing will be placed outside for sunlight disinfection.

3. Drink only boiled water. Do not eat uncooked food.

4. Cookhouses must be kept clean at all times.

5. All refuse deposited in sumps must be covered with earth and chloride of lime.

Appendix II

Glossary of Japanese words and phrases that it was compulsory for every prisoner to learn.

gentai go	Words of command
atsumare	Come here
kiotsuke	Attention
keirei	Salute
bango	Number
migie narae	Right dress
naore	Eyes front
seinmei	Total number
zikomei	Absent
genzai in moi	Present
tenko	Roll call
yasume	Stand at ease
zikono meiwa	Parade Statement
mei. keimei	Men. Total number
izyo arimasen	There is no change
zyunsatsu	Inspection
kyoren	Drill
tyumoko	Stand-at-ease
migimuke-migi	Right turn
hidarimuke-hidari	Left turn
maware migi	About turn
mae e susume	Quick march
hotyo tore (yame)	Ceremonial march
kasira migi, hidari	Eyes right, left
kasira migi, naka	Eyes front
butai temare	Halt

194

kisyo	Wake up
nittyo tenko	Morning roll call
tyo syoku	Breakfast
sagyo	Work
sagyo zyo	Working place
tyu syoku	Lunch
kyokei	Rest
kyoiku	Education
benkyo	Study
wundo	Physical training
wundo zyo	Playground
suiyoku	Bathwater
nisse ki tenko	Evening roll call
syu sin	Go to bed
syo to	Put out the lights
kuma	Hoe
baketsu	Buckets
hoki	Brush
tiri tori	Dustpan
kami	Paper
tetyo	Notebook
enpitsu	Pencil
heya	Room
roka	Verandah
sindai	Bed
mofu	Blanket
iriguchi	Entrance
kaidan	Step
suido	Water supply
dento	Electric light
takigi	Firewood
shio	Salt
mamo	Beans, Peas
niku	Meat
sate	Sugar

nasu	Brinjals
bosi	Hat
kutu	Footwear
tenko hayaku ike	Roll-call, let us go quickly
tenko gae watta taiseda	Roll call is finished, next physical training
soji o seyo	You sweep
hokio motte koi	Bring a dustpan here
hoki de hake	Sweep cleanly with a brush
Tiritori o motte koi	Bring a dustpan here
baketsu nimizue kundekoi	Bring water in buckets here
zokinde yaku o huke	Clean the floor with a cloth
shitunaiga kiroini natta	It is nice and clean in the room
shitunai no sciketu seitonni. yoku tyui seyo	Take care to clean and arrange the room
hai yoku tyui simasu	Yes, I will
minna kao o arae	All men, wash your faces
chayo. sayonara	Good-morning. Good-bye
mesi to akazue bunpai seye	Distribute your rice and food
hai sugu bunpai shimasu	Yes, I will certainly
tyo syoku ga owatta ka?	Did you finish breakfast?
syokugi ga sundara kyoronda	When breakfast is finished, begin training
imawa kyu koi zikanda	It is resting time now
yu syokuwa owari masita	Evening dinner is finished
suiyokumo owari masita	Also, bath water is finished too
zini syu des	10.30 p.m. is sleeping time
hanasie yamete neyo	Stop talking—go to sleep
ryomatu o terinikoi	Come here to fetch provisions
komeo motte iko	Take away the rice

Appendix III

GLOSSARY

A.D.M.S.	Assistant Director of Medical Services
A.D.S.	Advanced Dressing Station
A/Q	Adjutant and Quartermaster-General of a Division
A.T.	Animal Transport
B.A.M.C.	Burma Army Medical Corps
Benjo	Latrine
B.O.	British Officer
B.O.R.	British Other Rank
C.C.S.	Casualty Clearing Station
C.S.M.	Company Sergeant Major
Chaung	River bed
D.D.M.S.	Deputy Director of Medical Services
I.A.M.C.	Indian Army Medical Corps
I.A.T.	Inflammation of Areolar Tissue
I.M.S	Indian Medical Service
Juggeree	Coarse East Indian Sugar
M.I.	Medical Inspection
M.O.	Medical Officer
M.T.	Mechanical Transport
Moashi	Germinated Beans
Pongyii	Buddhist Monastery enclosure
V.C.O.	Viceroy's Commissioned Officer
W.O.	Warrant Officer

Appendix IV

Copy of a letter from the Japanese Medical Officer to each Medical Officer, imprisoned in Rangoon Jail.

My Dear Doktor!

I want to know about the Jungle Sore and I.A.T. concerning to officers and soldiers who has jungle sore and I.A.T. Please answer the following questions.

A. Name and age.
B. The body Weight before the War.
C. When began the Decease?
D. Where and Why? (for example) in Jungle, in the house, thrust through (pierce) by the branches of tree, etc.
E. Symptoms (The Detail of the Decease).

The Army Surgeon
Dr. Ikegami.

Appendix V

Copy of letter from Colonel Mackenzie to the Prison Commandant, asking for more food.

Sir,

I humbly and respectfully beg to submit the following for your consideration and help, regarding the health of the British Prisoners of War, which, in my opinion, is in a very low state at present, owing to under-nourishment and the results thereof.

The majority of the officers and men have now been prisoners in a tropical climate for periods varying from twenty months, without the normal amenities of life and generous diet to which they have been accustomed.

The present low state of general health is evident from the following:

(a) The high sickness rate due to I.A.T., scabies, ringworm of the body, beri-beri, failing eyesight and general debility.

(b) Very few men are able to perform two successive day's hard work, without having to report sick on account of exhaustion. They take several days to recover, and many develop malaria relapses, intestinal chills and colds in consequence, and are unable to build up any body reserves because of the diet. Lack of fresh meat in quantities to which we have been accustomed is one of the chief factors. Were the daily meat ration increased, and all of us are prepared to pay extra for this, the general level of health would be improved, and much of the present sickness would diminish or disappear altogether.

(c) A large number of men are so emaciated that they cannot be sent out on working parties. Several have been sent back to camp by Japanese sentries, as unfit to work.

(d) There have been about sixty deaths in this Block, apart from accidents and effects of wounds, since our first arrival.

(e) The men are all very willing to work and to do everything in their power they are asked to do, but when their physical strength and powers of endurance are exhausted, what can be expected of them?

I foresee that every month's continuance of prison life in the tropics, on a diet to which we are unaccustomed, can only increase the toll of deaths. We are not rice-eaters, like the majority of Indians and Burmans.

Might I suggest that a list of articles, which are available for purchase from the contractor be supplied to us monthly? This would help us to make out our ten-day orders.

Knowing the great interest you have in the welfare and treatment of Prisoners of War, I feel confident that you will use your influence to grant this request.

I have the honour to be,

Your obedient servant,

K. P. MacKenzie, Colonel.

Appendix VI

Copy of letter re Dixies in No. 3 Block Hospital Kitchen.

Sir,

I humbly and respectfully beg to point out that the hospital kitchen staff, at present, find it a matter of the greatest difficulty to cook the diets ordered for the hospital patients and the convalescents, on account of the state of the dixies. We have only one dixie that does not leak badly, and, although the leaks are stuffed with pieces of cloth every time they are used, they still do not answer the purpose.

I suggest, therefore, that to enable the hospital kitchen staff to provide all the diets ordered for the dysentery (*shekri*), beri-beri (*kakke*), and debility (*suijaku*) cases, etc., which average between 35 and 50, four new dixies, with lids, be provided.

I have the honour to be, Sir,

Your obedient servant,

K. P. MacKenzie, Colonel.

Author's Note.

This request is remarkable in that it was complied with immediately!